The Ultimate
Ninja Woodfire

Outdoor Grill & Smoker Cookbook for Beginners

2000-Day Ninja Woodfire Recipes for Backyard Barbecue, Family Gathering | Woodfire Flavor | Easy to Operate for Beginners

Margaret Voyles

Table of Contents

Welcome to the Ninja Woodfire outdoor grill cookbook! Outdoor cooking food can be very challenging. It is because you can't take all kinds of kitchen appliances and utensils when you are away from home. Now, you don't need to worry about it. Ninja Woodfire outdoor grill is a best appliance. It is a special recipe book to help you cook amazing food on a woodfire grill. It's like a magic book for cooking outside, making your meals taste fantastic.

Grilling is when we cook food on a grill, and this cookbook makes it extra fun by using Ninja woodfire, which gives a smoky and delicious flavor. It's like a campfire but for cooking yummy meals.

This book teaches you everything you need to know about Ninja woodfire grilling, like how to use different kinds of wood for flavor and how to control the grill's heat. It's like a guidebook for becoming a master at grilling.

Inside, you'll find many recipes for all kinds of foods, like juicy steaks, tasty burgers, fresh fish, and even desserts you can make on the grill. There are also recipes for yummy appetizers, side dishes, and sweet treats.

If you're new to grilling, don't worry! This book will show you step-by-step how to do it. And if you're already a grill expert, you'll still find new tricks and tips to make your food even better.

Whether you're cooking for a backyard barbecue, a family gathering, or a cozy evening under the stars, the "Ninja Woodfire Outdoor Grill Cookbook" will empower you to create unforgettable outdoor dining experiences. So, put on your cooking apron, light up the woodfire grill, and let this cookbook be your friend in making delicious outdoor meals. You'll amaze your family and friends with the tasty food you can create using the Ninja Woodfire Outdoor Grill Cookbook!

What is Ninja Woodfire Pro XL Outdoor Grill?

Ninja Woodfire outdoor grill is an innovative outdoor cooking appliance designed to bring an authentic flavor of wood-fired cooking to your backyard. It is a versatile cooking appliance that offers high performance to enhance your outdoor cooking experience. It is designed to provide exceptional results, and it is perfect for various cooking styles and dishes. It has a power convection fan and integrated smoke box, specially designed for Ninja Woodfire pellets to create a rich, fully developed woodfire pellet.

Woodfire outdoor grill is a potential game changer. From searing to smoking to roasting, this grill improves your cooking skills and gives you extraordinary yield. In addition, the natural flavors of the wood pellets enhance the taste of your meals, giving them a delicious, smoky profile that will delight your taste buds.

It provides a safe and relaxed environment. It comes in different flavors. Adjust the cooking temperature easily with a dial, and once the grill reaches the desired temperature, place food onto the grill grate. The conduction fan circulates the smoke, disturbing the heat evenly and cooking food perfectly. One of the best things about this grill is how easy it is to start!

You will get breakfast, lunch, dinner, and dessert recipes from my cookbook. You can select recipes for the whole day and prepare them for your family. It is a safe and versatile appliance and perfect for making delicious food. Let's discuss more about this appliance. So, without any more delay, let's jump right in and start exploring the fundamentals of your appliance.

Cooking Functions:
Grill, Smoker, Air Crisp, Bake, Roast, Broil, and Dehydrate
Essential Parts:
Grill Grate, Crisper Basket, Smoke Box, Grease Tray, Left and Right Assembly Handles, Socket Head Cap Screw, Allen Wrench, Pellet Scoop, Assembled Main Unit (power cord not shown), Hood, Control Panel
Operating Buttons:
Dial, Woodfire flavor technology, Temperature, Time, Start/Stop

Before First Use

- Discard all packaging material and tape from the unit. Also, remove all accessories from the package.
- Please pay attention to instructions and necessary safeguards to protect from injury and damage.
- Rinse the crisper basket and grill grate in soapy and warm water. Then, rinse and dry thoroughly.
- Some accessories, such as grill grate, base unit, and crisper basket, are not dishwasher safe. Never clean the main unit in the dishwasher.
- Don't use abrasive brushes or sponges on the cooking surface. Otherwise, it will damage the surface.

Main functions of Ninja woodfire outdoor grill

Grill

Grilling outdoor is an amazing feeling. Grill your favorite food like chicken, beef, pork, lamb, seafood, veggies, and many more. Using the closed hood ensures that the food

is cooked evenly from both the top and bottom, making it ideal for grilling large or thick cuts of meat, frozen food, or achieving a thorough sear overall. Open the hood while grilling delicate foods or lean proteins to develop char-grilled textures without overcooking.

How to use:

- Position the grill on a stable, flat surface.
- Lift the grill hood and set the grill grate on top of the heating element, ensuring it sits securely in place.
- Slide the grease tray into position at the back of the grill.
- If you intend to utilize the Woodfire Flavor Technology, raise the smoke box lid and fill it with Ninja Woodfire Pellets using the pellet scoop, making sure not to overfill it. Close the lid.
- Ensure the grill is plugged in, and turn the dial clockwise from the OFF position to select the GRILL function.
- If you're adding Woodfire Flavor, press the WOODFIRE FLAVOR button. The default temperature setting will be shown; you can adjust it using the - and + buttons next to TEMP.
- To modify the cooking time, use the - and + buttons next to TIME.
- Press START to commence the preheating process. If you're using Woodfire Flavor technology, the pellets will go through an ignition cycle (IGN), and then the grill will start preheating (PRE).
- Once preheating is finished, the unit will emit a beep, and the display will show "ADD FOOD."
- Open the hood and place your ingredients on the grill grate. After closing the hood, the cooking process will start, and the timer will begin counting down.
- When the cooking time reaches zero, the grill will beep, and "DONE" will appear on the display.
- Remove your food from the grill grate.

Smoker

Smoking food is a method of cooking that involves exposing it to smoke from burning wood, which imparts a smoky flavor. Common foods for smoking include meats like ribs, brisket, and fish. To smoke food, you'll need a smoker or grill with a lid, wood chips or chunks for smoking, and patience, as it's a slow-cooking process.

How to use:

- Position the grill on a flat, level surface. Open the grill hood and place the grill grate flat on top of the heating element to secure it in place. Slide the grease tray into position at the back of the grill.
- Lift the lid of the smoke box and use the pellet scoop to fill it with Ninja Woodfire Pellets up to the top level. Be careful not to overflow the smoke box.
- Open the grill hood and arrange your ingredients on the grill grate, then close the hood.
- Ensure the grill is plugged in and turn the dial clockwise from the OFF position to select the SMOKER function.
- The default temperature setting will be displayed. To adjust the temperature, if desired, use the - and + buttons located next to TEMP.
- To adjust the cooking time, use the - and + buttons next to TIME. Press the START button to initiate the cooking process. There's no need for a preheat time with the Smoker function.
- When the cooking time reaches zero, the grill will beep, and the display will show "END." Remove your food from the grill grate.

Air Crisp

Air crisp cooking is used to make the food crispy and crunchy in less-to-no oil. It gives the food the perfect texture and yummy flavor. We recommend this cooking function for Frozen food, French fries, chicken nuggets, fish sticks, pizza, rolls, tater tots, and casseroles. If you have leftover food, you can reheat it using the air crisp function. It gives you a crispy and brown texture.

How to use:

- Position the grill on a flat, level surface. Open the grill hood and securely place the grill grate on top of the heating element.
- Set the crisper basket onto the grill grate and align the basket feet with the designated indentations on the grill grate surface. Slide the grease tray into position at the back of the grill.
- If you intend to use the Woodfire Flavor Technology, lift the smoke box lid and, using the pellet scoop, fill the smoke box with Ninja Woodfire Pellets up to the top level. Ensure not to overflow the smoke box.
- Make sure the grill is plugged in and turn the dial clockwise from the OFF position to select the AIR CRISP function.
- If you plan to add woodfire flavor, press the WOODFIRE FLAVOR technology button. The default temperature setting will be displayed. Adjust the temperature if desired using the - and + buttons next to TEMP. To modify the cooking time, use the - and + buttons next to TIME.
- Press the START button to commence the preheating process. If utilizing Woodfire Flavor technology, the pellets will go through an ignition cycle (IGN), and then the grill will start preheating (PRE).
- When the preheating is finished, the grill will beep, and the display will show "ADD FOOD." Open the hood and arrange your ingredients on the grill grate. Once the hood is closed, cooking will initiate, and the timer will start counting down.
- When the cooking time reaches zero, the grill will beep, and "DONE" will appear on the display. Retrieve your food from the crisper basket.

Bake

With the bake cooking function, you can bake pies, cakes, muffins, cupcakes, casseroles, brownies, and other your favorite baked items. With lower fan speed, you can bake your favorite foods. Baking at a lower temperature for a longer time avoids burning and too much browning of the foods. Bake is the perfect option for making treats for your kids.

How to use:

- Set the grill on a flat, even surface. Open the hood and position the grill grate flat on the heating element to secure it in place.
- Slide the grease tray into position at the back of the grill. If you intend to use the Woodfire Flavor Technology, raise the smoke box lid and use the pellet scoop to fill the smoke box with Ninja Woodfire Pellets up to the top, then close the lid. Avoid overflowing the smoke box.
- Ensure the grill is plugged in and turn the dial clockwise from the OFF position to choose the BAKE function.
- If incorporating woodfire flavor, press the WOODFIRE FLAVOR button. The default temperature setting will be visible. To adjust the temperature if needed, use the − and + buttons next to TEMP. Adjust the cook time using the - and + buttons next to TIME.
- Press START to initiate preheating. If utilizing Woodfire Flavor technology, the pellets will go through an ignition cycle (IGN), and then the grill will start preheating (PRE).
- Once preheating is complete, the unit will beep, and "ADD FOOD" will appear on the display. Open the hood and arrange ingredients on the grill grate or place the bake pan on the grate. Once the hood is closed, cooking will start, and the

timer will commence counting down.

- When the cook time reaches zero, the grill will beep, and "DONE" will appear on the display. Take out your food from the grill grate.

Roast

With the roast option, you can prepare roasted chicken, lamb, fish, pork, vegetables, etc. Roast cooking functions give tender, delicious, and juicy meals. We recommend this cooking function for meats and vegetables. The roast cooking option provides the food with crispness, a ton of flavors, browning tops, and tendering the foods. You didn't need to buy an oven to roast the meats.

How to use:

- Set the grill on a flat, even surface. Open the hood and position the grill grate flat on the heating element to secure it in place.
- Slide the grease tray into position at the back of the grill. If you intend to use the Woodfire Flavor Technology, raise the smoke box lid and use the pellet scoop to fill the smoke box with Ninja Woodfire Pellets up to the top, and then close the lid. Avoid overflowing the smoke box.
- Ensure the grill is plugged in and turn the dial clockwise from the OFF position to choose the ROAST function.
- If incorporating woodfire flavor, press the WOODFIRE FLAVOR button. The default temperature setting will be visible. To adjust the temperature if needed, use the – and + buttons next to TEMP. Adjust the cook time using the - and + buttons next to TIME.
- Press START to initiate preheating. If utilizing Woodfire Flavor technology, the pellets will go through an ignition cycle (IGN), and then the grill will start preheating (PRE).
- Once preheating is complete, the unit will beep, and "ADD FOOD" will appear on the display. Open the hood and arrange ingredients on the grill grate. Once the hood is closed, cooking will start, and the timer will commence counting down.
- When the cook time reaches zero, the grill will beep, and "DONE" will appear on the display. Take out your food from the grill grate.

Broil

When using the BROIL cooking function, the heat source comes from the top, allowing you to add quick finishing crisply. You can use the broil cooking function for broiling veggies, fruits, and meats. It gives caramelized, seared, and juicy food.

How to use:

- Set the grill on a flat, even surface. Open the hood and position the grill grate flat on the heating element to secure it in place.
- Place the grease tray into position by sliding it into the slot located at the rear of the unit.
- Open the hood and place ingredients on the grill grate. Close the hood. There is no preheating.
- Make sure the unit is plugged in and rotate the dial clockwise from the OFF position to select the BROIL function.
- The default temperature setting will display. To adjust temperature if needed, use the - and + buttons next to TEMP.
- To adjust cook time, use the - and + buttons next to TIME. Press START to begin cooking.
- When cook time reaches zero, the unit will beep and DONE will appear on the display. Remove food from the grill grate.

Dehydrate

Dehydrate cooking function removes the moisture from the foods. Using this cooking option, you can preserve the food for a long time. It takes a long time to cook food, but it gives you tender and delicious food. We recommend this cooking function to make jerky or dehydrating fruits or veggies, jerky beef, etc.

How to use:

- Set the grill on a flat, even surface.
- Open the hood and install the grill grate by positioning it flat on top

of the heating element so it sits into place.
- Install the grease tray by sliding it into place at the back of the unit.
- Open the hood and place ingredients on the grill grate. Close the hood. There is no preheating.
- Make sure the unit is plugged in and rotate the dial clockwise from the OFF position to select the "DEHYDRATE" function.
- The default temperature setting will display. To adjust temperature if needed, use the - and + buttons next to TEMP.
- To adjust cook time, use the - and + buttons next to TIME.
- Press START to begin cooking.
- When cook time reaches zero, the unit will beep and DONE will appear on the display. Remove food from the grill grate.

Woodfire Flavor Technology

- To add Woodfire Flavor, after step 3, lift the smoke box lid and fill the smoke box with Ninja Woodfire Pellets to the top, then close the lid. DO NOT overflow the smoke box.
- Skip step 4, and follow steps 5–7 for programming. Press the WOODFIRE FLAVOR button after you select DEHYDRATES in step 4.
- After step 7, press START to begin preheating. The pellets will go through an ignition cycle (IGN).
- When preheating is complete, the grill will beep and ADD FOOD will appear on the display.
- Open the hood and place the ingredients on the grill grate. Once the hood is closed, cooking will start, and the timer will start counting down.
- When cook time reaches zero, the grill will beep, and DONE will appear on the display. Remove food from the grill grate.

Tips and Tricks of Using It
- While cooking food, no needs to refuel just add one full scoop of pellet into the smoke box.
- Don't use woodfire flavor technology with frozen foods.
- Certain foods such as veggies may absorb smoky flavor than others.

Operating Buttons

Dial:
To turn on the unit, choose a cooking function; rotate the dial clockwise until the dial is shown to the desired cooking function. To turn off the unit, rotate the dial counterclockwise to the OFF position.
Note: The display will be illuminated when the unit is turned on.

Woodfire Flavor Technology:
Press after choosing your cooking function to add Woodfire flavor using the Grill, Air Crisp, Bake, Roast, or Dehydrate functions. When pressed, the flame icon will illuminate on the display screen.

Temperature:
To adjust the temperature, the display will show the default temperature. Use the – and + buttons next to TEMP.

Time:
Use the – and + buttons next to TIME to adjust the cooking time.

START/STOP:
Press the start or stop button to start the cooking function. Press and hold for 4 seconds to skip preheat.

Preheat for Better Results:
For best grilling results, preheat the appliance before adding the food. Then, add food before preheating is complete. It

may lead to overcooking, smoke and longer preheating time. After you adjust the cooking function, time, and temperature, press START, and the unit will automatically begin preheating (except if using the Smoker function or the Broil/Dehydrate functions without enabling Woodfire Flavor Technology).

Benefits of Using this Appliance

Multi-functional cooking pot:

The ninja woodfire outdoor grill cooking appliance has 7 cooking functions in one pot: grill, smoke, air crisp, roast, broil, bake, and dehydrate. You don't need to buy another appliance for baking cakes, dehydrating fruits and meat, or air-frying foods. You will find all types of cooking functions in one pot.

Grilling at home:

Grilling at home presents a wonderful opportunity to enjoy the rich flavors of outdoor cooking. Whether you're a seasoned grill master or a beginner, there's a vast array of culinary delights to explore, ranging from timeless favorites like burgers and steaks to inventive creations like grilled vegetables and pizzas. Don't forget safety precautions, keep your grill clean, and enjoy the process of creating delicious meals right in your backyard.

Tips for Using Accessories

Non-Stick Grill Grate:

The grill grate is used for every cooking function. In this grill grate, six burgers, 30 hot dogs, and two racks of ribs could fit. Set the grill on a flat, even surface. Open the hood or lid and install the grill grate by adjusting it flat on top of the heating element so it sits in place.

Flat-Top Griddle Plate:

Using a flat-top griddle plate, you can make tortillas, pancakes, patties, and fajitas.

Crisper Basket:

A crisper basket is used in air fry, roast, dehydrate, and broil cooking functions. You can add 3 pounds of food at the same time into the crisper basket.

Grill Cover:

Grill cover is very important when pouring rain and scorching sun. The grill cover is durable, lightweight, and water-resistant. It keeps the appliance safe.

Pellet Scoop:

It is designed to measure the perfect amount of Ninja Woodfire pellet.

Removable Woodfire Smoke Box:

It comes fully installed into the appliance. Before adding the pellet, insert it into the position.

Grease Tray:

Before every cooking process, always insert the grease tray.

Cleaning process of Ninja Woodfire Outdoor Grill

- Rinse the grill grate thoroughly after each use. Allow the appliance and accessories to cool before cleaning.
- Before cleaning, unplug the grill from the power source. Keep the hood open after removing your food to expedite cooling. Safely discard all contents from the smoke box after each use.
- The pellet scoop is dishwasher safe, but the grill grate, crisper basket, grease tray, and smoke box are not.
- Carefully remove the cooled grease tray from the back of the unit and safely discard grease contents after each use. You should wash the grease tray in warm and soapy water.
- Cleaning the smoke box is optional, but a wire brush can remove extra creosote if desired. Wipe down the inner hood

with a damp towel or cloth after each use to deodorize the unit and remove any grease.

- If food residue or grease is stuck on the grill grate or any other removable part, soak it in warm, soapy water before cleaning.
- Remove the non-stick grill grate and non-stick crisper basket (if used) after each use and hand-wash with warm, soapy water. Gently wipe down the inside of the hood with a damp cloth.
- When stacking the coated accessories for storage, place a cloth or paper towel between each piece to protect the coated surfaces.

Troubleshooting

The panel display appears "ADD FOOD" on its screen.
When the unit is complete preheating then the display shows "ADD FOOD" on its screen. So, it is time to add food into the crisper basket or grill grate.
The panel display appears "CLOSE HOOD" on its screen.
It is showed when the hood remains open and need to be close for choosing function to start cooking.
The panel display appears "ADD GRILL" on its screen.
The grill grate needs to be installed. Once installed, closed the hood and press the Start button to begin.
The panel display appears "E" on its screen.
It is showed when the unit is not functioning properly. You can contact with care customer service.
Should I add the ingredients before or after preheating?
If you want best results, allow the unit to preheat before adding ingredients.
Should I use any oils or non-stick sprays when smoking?

No, we didn't recommend using any oils or cooking spray when smoking because smoke will not adhere to the food as well.
Why is preheat taking so long?
Grill takes approximately 12 to 20 minutes for preheating
Air Crisp, Bake, and Roast take 3 minutes for preheating
Smoker, dehydrate, and Broil take no preheat.

Important Safety Instructions

- Don't use heating fuel pellets, charcoal, liquid fuels, hardwood, and any other combustible material into the smoker.
- When the smoker is hot, ensure hands and face is kept away from the smoker box. Always have a fire extinguisher within reach while using the smoker.
- Store wood pellets in a dry place, away from heat sources and other fuel containers.
- Maintain a clean grill; prevent grease and ash buildup to avoid grease fires and unwanted smoke affecting food flavor. Refer to the Cleaning & Maintenance section for routine appliance care. To disconnect, power off, unplug, and store indoors when not in use.
- Avoid cleaning the product with water sprays or metal scouring pads to prevent electric shock risks. Keep the grill covered when stored outdoors to protect it from the elements and always store indoors, out of children's reach.

4-Week Meal Plan

Week 1

Day 1:
Breakfast: Cheese Pancetta Frittata
Lunch: Lemony Asparagus with Almonds
Snack: Creamy Smoked Onion Dip
Dinner: Smoky Whole Chicken
Dessert: Cinnamon Chocolate Sauce

Day 2:
Breakfast: Homemade Pita Bread
Lunch: Balsamic Brussels Sprouts & Bacon
Snack: Cheese Pulled Pork Potato Skins
Dinner: Mustard-Smoked Salmon Steaks
Dessert: Lemon Peach Cobbler

Day 3:
Breakfast: Grilled Naan
Lunch: Smoked Chantilly Potatoes
Snack: Cheese Bacon Egg Pizza
Dinner: Herbed Rack of Lamb
Dessert: Best Apple Crisp

Day 4:
Breakfast: Smoked Paprika Deviled Eggs
Lunch: Homemade Holiday Stuffing
Snack: Easy Grilled Pineapple and Peaches
Dinner: Smoked Sweet Turkey Legs
Dessert: Homemade Candied Pineapple

Day 5:
Breakfast: Grilled Shakshouka
Lunch: Easy Smoked Butternut Squash
Snack: Grilled Flatbread
Dinner: Smoked Halibut and Mushrooms
Dessert: Soft Ginger Cake

Day 6:
Breakfast: Country Sausage Baked Beans
Lunch: BBQ Sauce Smoked Beans
Snack: Fiesta Shrimp Salsa with Tortilla Chips
Dinner: Lamb Cheeseburgers
Dessert: Chocolate Bread Pudding

Day 7:
Breakfast: Butternut Squash-Bacon Bread Pudding
Lunch: Caramelized Onions
Snack: Simple Smoked Eggs
Dinner: Honey Mustard Smoked Pulled Pork
Dessert: Flavorful Pumpkin Pie

Week 2

Day 1:
Breakfast: Asparagus Tomato Frittata
Lunch: Grilled Cajun Corn on the Cob
Snack: Shrimp Kebabs with Rémoulade
Dinner: Delicious Caramelized Orange Duck
Dessert: Pineapple & Cherry Upside-Down Cake

Day 2:
Breakfast: Basic Bread
Lunch: Cheese Jalapeño Corn Bread
Snack: Peach and Blue Cheese Bruschetta
Dinner: Lemon Crab Cakes with Remoulade Sauce
Dessert: Banana Chocolate Sundaes

Day 3:
Breakfast: Mexican-Style Green Chile–Cheese Corn Bread
Lunch: Grilled Chimichurri Eggplant
Snack: Filet Mignon Crostini
Dinner: Mustard Curry-Rubbed Leg of Lamb
Dessert: Raisins Stuffed Apples

Day 4:
Breakfast: Garlic-Butter Bread
Lunch: Grilled Vegetable Kebabs
Snack: Grilled Bacon-Wrapped Jalapeño Poppers
Dinner: Apricot Jam-Glazed Cornish Game Hens
Dessert: Mixed Berries Crisp

Day 5:
Breakfast: Homemade Breakfast Pork Sausage
Lunch: Grilled Garlic Polenta
Snack: Hot Smoked Almonds
Dinner: Lemon-Herb Roasted Whole Trout
Dessert: Cherry Hand Pies

Day 6:
Breakfast: Cheese Pancetta Frittata
Lunch: Roasted Sweet Potato Slices
Snack: Crispy Russet Potato Fries
Dinner: Smoked Venison Steaks with Blackberry Sauce
Dessert: Roasted Strawberry Ice Cream

Day 7:
Breakfast: Grilled Naan
Lunch: Honey-Bourbon Glazed Carrots
Snack: Spicy Chicken Skewers with Honey-Lime Cream
Dinner: Smoked Sweet Ham
Dessert: Delicious S'mores

Week 3

Day 1:
Breakfast: Smoked Paprika Deviled Eggs
Lunch: Savory Bacon with Brussels Sprouts
Snack: Cheesy Crab and Artichoke Dip
Dinner: Roasted Garlic Turkey
Dessert: Cinnamon Chocolate Sauce

Day 2:
Breakfast: Fluffy Cornbread
Lunch: Smoked Heirloom Carrots & Jalapeño
Snack: Spicy Garlic Shrimp
Dinner: Garlic Lobster Tails with Drawn Butter
Dessert: Homemade Pineapple Upside-Down Cake

Day 3:
Breakfast: Grilled Shakshouka
Lunch: Herb-Smoked Potatoes with Goose Fat
Snack: Sweet & Sour Chicken Wings
Dinner: Yummy Lamb Kebabs
Dessert: Lemon Peach Cobbler

Day 4:
Breakfast: Country Sausage Baked Beans
Lunch: Smoked Potatoes with Shallots
Snack: Cheese Jalapeño Stuffed Mushrooms
Dinner: Grilled Spiced Chicken
Dessert: Best Apple Crisp

Day 5:
Breakfast: Homemade Pita Bread
Lunch: Homemade Pico De Gallo
Snack: Baked Buffalo Chicken Nachos
Dinner: Garlic Lobster Tails with Drawn Butter
Dessert: Homemade Candied Pineapple

Day 6:
Breakfast: Butternut Squash-Bacon Bread Pudding
Lunch: Spicy Garlic Black Beans
Snack: Roasted Chipotle-Rubbed Chicken Wings
Dinner: Pineapple-Flavored Venison Loin Roast
Dessert: Chocolate Bread Pudding

Day 7:
Breakfast: Asparagus Tomato Frittata
Lunch: Refreshing Cabbage Slaw
Snack: Cheese Sausage-Stuffed Jalapeños
Dinner: Texas Pork Steaks
Dessert: Soft Ginger Cake

Week 4

Day 1:
Breakfast: Homemade Breakfast Pork Sausage
Lunch: Smoked Cheesy Hash Brown Potatoes
Snack: Hot and Sweet Chicken Wings
Dinner: Delicious Thanksgiving Turkey
Dessert: Flavorful Pumpkin Pie

Day 2:
Breakfast: Honey Corn Bread
Lunch: Cheese Corn Pudding
Snack: Cheese Bacon Egg Pizza
Dinner: Smoked Peppercorn Littleneck Clams
Dessert: Banana Chocolate Sundaes

Day 3:
Breakfast: Cheese Pancetta Frittata
Lunch: Grilled Zucchini with Basil & Orange Zest
Snack: Savory Turkey Meatballs
Dinner: Lamb-Mushroom Burgers
Dessert: Pineapple & Cherry Upside-Down Cake

Day 4:
Breakfast: Grilled Naan
Lunch: Roasted Carrots Salad
Snack: Cheesy Steak & Black Beans Nachos
Dinner: Aromatic Tea-Smoked Whole Duck
Dessert: Raisins Stuffed Apples

Day 5:
Breakfast: Mexican-Style Green Chile–Cheese Corn Bread
Lunch: Grilled Corn Ears
Snack: Roasted Garlic Potatoes
Dinner: Spicy Shrimp Tostadas
Dessert: Mixed Berries Crisp

Day 6:
Breakfast: Smoked Paprika Deviled Eggs
Lunch: Tasty Jerk-Marinated Tofu
Snack: Grilled Watermelon Wedges with Feta
Dinner: Garlicky Lamb Chops
Dessert: Cherry Hand Pies

Day 7:
Breakfast: Garlic-Butter Bread
Lunch: Mint Beet Salad
Snack: Cheese Pulled Pork Potato Skins
Dinner: Lemony Pork Kebabs
Dessert: Roasted Strawberry Ice Cream

Chapter 1 Breakfast Recipes

Grilled Naan

Prep Time: 20 minutes | Cook Time: 6 minutes | Serves: 14

1 (¼-ounce) package active dry yeast
1 cup warm water (105° to 110° F)
¼ cup sugar
3 tablespoons whole milk
1 large egg, beaten
2 teaspoons regular table salt, not kosher

2 cups whole wheat flour
2½ cups bread flour
¼ cup (½ stick) unsalted butter, melted
Kosher salt
Middle Eastern Za'tar Seasoning, optional

1. In the bowl of a stand mixer fitted with a dough hook, dissolve the yeast in the warm water and let rest until frothy, about 10 minutes. On low speed, mix in the sugar, milk, egg, regular salt, and whole wheat flour. As that mixes, slowly add in the bread flour. Turn the mixer speed up one notch and let the machine knead the dough for 6 to 8 minutes, until you have a smooth dough that attaches itself to the dough hook. 2. Transfer the dough to a greased bowl. Then cover it with a damp cloth and let rise until doubled in volume, about 1 hour. 3. Punch down the dough and pinch off golf ball–size portions. Roll these into balls and place in a baking sheet. Cover with a clean kitchen towel and let rise until doubled in size, about 30 minutes. 4. To install grill grate, position it flat on top of the heating element so it sits in place, then close hood. Use pellet scoop to pour pellets into smoke box until filled to top. 5. Select GRILL. Select WOODFIRE FLAVOR. Set grill temperature to HI. Set the time to 6 minutes. Select START/STOP to begin preheating. 6. On a floured work surface with a floured rolling pin, roll each ball of dough into a circle about ¼ inch thick. 7. When unit beeps to signify it has preheated and ADD FOOD displays, open hood and place as many pieces of dough as will fit on the grill grate. Close hood and grill for 6 minutes, flipping halfway through. Grill until nicely browned. 8. As you remove the naan from the grill grate, brush with the butter and sprinkle with kosher salt and za'tar if using. Continue until all the naan has been grilled. You can freeze the dough for later use if desired. Just let the balls thaw and rise before cooking. Naan is best eaten hot but you can store leftovers in a zip-top bag for a couple of days; just reheat in your oven before serving.

Smoked Paprika Deviled Eggs

Prep Time: 10 minutes | Cook Time: minutes | Serves: 6

½ cup mayonnaise
½ cup yellow mustard
Kosher salt

Freshly ground black pepper
1 teaspoon paprika

1. Gently place the eggs in a large pot and cover with water. Bring to a boil, then reduce the heat to low and simmer for 10 minutes. Turn the stove off and let the eggs sit in the hot water for 45 minutes. 2. Place a few ice cubes in the water with the eggs to cool them slightly, but they should still be warm and easy to peel. Peel the eggs. 3. To install the grill grate, position it flat on top of the heating element so it sits in place. 4. Place the eggs on the grill grate, then close the hood. 5. Use the pellet scoop to pour pellets into the smoke box until filled to the top. Select SMOKER. Set grill temperature to 180°F and time to 45 minutes. Select START/STOP to begin cooking. 6. Once done cooking, cut the eggs in half lengthwise, remove the yolks, and put the yolks in a large bowl. Place the whites, cut-side up, on a tray. 7. In the bowl containing the egg yolks, combine the mayonnaise, mustard, along with a pinch of salt and pepper. Use a hand mixer to beat the mixture for 1 minute, then taste it to adjust the seasoning if necessary. Distribute this mixture evenly among the egg white halves. 8. Sprinkle with the paprika and store in the refrigerator until ready to serve.

Homemade Pita Bread

Prep Time: 25 minutes | Cook Time: 6 minutes | Serves: 12

1½ cups unbleached all-purpose flour
½ cup whole wheat flour
2 teaspoons regular table salt, not kosher

2 teaspoons instant yeast
2 tablespoons olive oil
1¼ cups warm water (105° to 110° F)

1. Make the dough at least 1½ hours before baking. This will yield better flavor. In the bowl of a stand mixer fitted with a paddle attachment, combine all of the ingredients and mix on low speed until the flour is fully moistened. This will take less than a minute. Change to the dough hook and let the machine run on medium speed for about 10 minutes. The dough will clean the bowl and be smooth, soft, and a little sticky. 2. Spray the inside of a large bowl with cooking spray. Place the dough in the bowl and lightly spray the top. Cover it with plastic wrap and let rise at room temperature until the dough doubles in size. This will take about 1½ hours, but you can let the dough continue to rise for up to 8 hours. You can refrigerate the risen dough for up to 3 days. 3. Move the dough onto a work surface lightly dusted with flour and divide it into 8 to 12 equal portions. Work with one portion at a time while keeping the others covered with a moist cloth. Shape each portion into a ball and then press it down into a disk shape. Cover the dough with plastic wrap sprayed with cooking spray and let rest for 20 minutes at room temperature. 4. To install the grill grate, position it flat on top of the heating element so it sits in place. 5. Roll each disc into a circle about ¼ inch thick. Allow them to rest for 10 minutes, uncovered, before baking. 6. Select the BAKE function. Adjust the temperature to 475°F and time to 6 minutes. Select START/STOP to begin preheating. 7. When preheating is complete, open the hood and place as many pieces of dough on the grate, about an inch apart. Once the hood is closed, cooking will begin and the timer will start counting down. Bake for 6 minutes, flipping them halfway through. They may puff up during cooking; if they do, flatten them with a spatula. 8. When cook time reaches zero, the grill will beep and DONE will appear on the display. Remove food from grill grate. 9. Transfer the baked pitas to a clean kitchen towel and wrap them up. Continue until all the pitas are baked. Serve hot or, when completely cool, store in a zip-top plastic bag for up to 3 days or in the freezer for up to 2 months.

Basic Bread

Prep Time: 15 minutes | Cook Time: 45 minutes | Serves: 4

3 cups unbleached all-purpose flour
2 teaspoons regular table salt, not kosher

1 teaspoon active dry yeast
12/3 cups warm water (105° to 110° F)

1. In a large bowl, combine the flour, salt, and yeast and mix well. Stir in the water until you have a very sticky, shaggy-looking dough. Cover with plastic wrap and let rise in the refrigerator for 18 to 24 hours. 2. Flour the work surface. Remove the plastic wrap from the bowl. The dough will have risen and be covered with bubbles. Transfer the dough to the work surface and dust the top with flour. Fold the dough in half, form it into a ball by stretching and tucking the edges of the dough underneath it. Flour a kitchen towel and place the dough on it. Top with another floured towel; let rise until doubled in size, about 2 hours. 3. To install the grill grate, position it flat on top of the heating element so it sits in place. 4. Select the BAKE function. Adjust the temperature to 450°F and time to 30 minutes. Select START/STOP to begin preheating. 5. Gently turn the dough ball onto a baking pan, seam side down. 6. When preheating is complete, open the hood and place the baking pan on the grill grate. Once the hood is closed, cooking will begin and the timer will start counting down. Then flip and continue to bake until the crust is golden brown, 15 to 20 minutes. 7. Transfer the bread to a wire rack and let cool before slicing—if you can wait that long.

Fluffy Cornbread

Prep Time: 10 minutes | Cook Time: 25 minutes | Serves: 8

2 cups self-rising cornmeal mix
11/3 cups buttermilk
¼ cup corn oil

1 large egg, slightly beaten
1 to 2 tablespoons sugar

1. Spray a baking pan with 2-inch sides with cooking spray. 2. To install the grill grate, position it flat on top of the heating element so it sits in place. 3. Select the BAKE function. Adjust the temperature to 375°F and time to 25 minutes. Select START/STOP to begin preheating. 4. In a large bowl, whisk the cornmeal mix, buttermilk, oil, egg, and sugar, if using, together. 5. Pour the batter into the baking pan. When preheating is complete, open the hood and place the baking pan on the grate. Once the hood is closed, cooking will begin and the timer will start counting down. Bake until the cornbread pulls away from the side of the pan and a toothpick inserted in the center comes out clean. 6. Remove the pan from the grill grate, cut the cornbread into 8 wedges or squares, and serve hot.

Cheese Pancetta Frittata

Prep Time: 10 minutes | Cook Time: 40 minutes | Serves: 6

8 large eggs
2 tablespoons milk
1 cup shredded fontina cheese
Kosher salt and freshly ground black pepper

1 tablespoon unsalted butter
½ cup diced onion
4 ounces pancetta, diced
¼ cup sour cream for serving (optional)

1. To install the grill grate, position it flat on top of the heating element so it sits in place. 2. Select the BAKE function. Adjust the temperature to 400°F and time to 25 minutes. Select START/STOP to begin preheating. 3. In a large bowl, whisk the eggs, milk, salt, cheese and pepper to taste together. 4. In a cast-iron skillet over medium heat, melt the butter; when it foams, add the onion and cook until it is soft and some color develops, about 10 minutes, stirring occasionally. Add the pancetta and cook, stirring a few times, until it takes on a little color, about 5 minutes. Pour the egg mixture into the baking pan and stir it around with a spatula so that the eggs make full contact with the bottom of the pan. 5. When preheating is complete, open the hood and place the baking pan on the grate. Once the hood is closed, cooking will begin and the timer will start counting down. Bake until the frittata is puffed up and golden brown. 6. Remove the pan from the grill grate and let cool for about 10 minutes. Slice the frittata into wedges and serve with sour cream, if desired.

Country Sausage Baked Beans

Prep Time: 10 minutes | Cook Time: 1 hour| Serves: 10

3 (32-ounce) cans pork and beans, drained
2 pounds country breakfast sausage, browned and crumbled
2 medium onions, thinly sliced into half moons
1 cup firmly packed light brown sugar

1 cup dark corn syrup
¼ cup prepared yellow mustard
1 tablespoon dry mustard
2 teaspoons Worcestershire sauce

1. To install the grill grate, position it flat on top of the heating element so it sits in place. 2. Select the BAKE function. Adjust the temperature to 350°F and time to 1 hour. Select START/STOP to begin preheating. 3. Pour the drained pork and beans in a disposable aluminum-foil baking pan. Add the sausage and onions and stir to mix. Add the remaining ingredients and stir to blend well. 4. When preheating is complete, open the hood and place the baking pan on the grate. Once the hood is closed, cooking will begin and the timer will start counting down.

Asparagus Tomato Frittata

Prep Time: 20 minutes | Cook Time: 20 minutes | Serves: 6

6 large eggs
¼ cup half-and-half
¼ cup freshly grated Parmigiano-Reggiano® cheese (scant 1 ounce)
¼ teaspoon kosher salt
¼ teaspoon freshly ground black pepper

1 tablespoon extra-virgin olive oil
2 garlic cloves, finely chopped
1 cup ripe cherry tomatoes, cut in half crosswise
6 ounces feta cheese, crumbled (scant 1¼ cups)

1. Take each asparagus spear individually and hold it at one end. Gently bend it until it breaks naturally at its tender point, typically around two-thirds down from the tip. Remove and discard the tough ends. Then, cut the spears diagonally into 1-inch pieces. Set them aside for later use. 2. In a blender combine the eggs, half-and-half, Parmigiano-Reggiano®, salt, and black pepper and process for 10 seconds to blend thoroughly. Set aside. 3. To install grill grate, position it flat on top of the heating element so it sits in place, then close hood. Use pellet scoop to pour pellets into smoke box until filled to top. 4. Select GRILL. Select WOODFIRE FLAVOR. Set grill temperature to LO. Set the time to 15 minutes. Select START/STOP to begin preheating. 5. Preheat a nonstick skillet over direct medium heat for 3 minutes. Add the oil to the skillet and then add the asparagus and stir briefly to coat with the oil. Cook with the lid closed, for 2 minutes. 6. Coat the bottom and sides of a baking pan with oil. Arrange the asparagus in an even layer, and then scatter the garlic, tomatoes, and feta evenly over the asparagus. Pour the egg mixture into the pan. 7. When unit beeps to signify it has preheated and ADD FOOD displays, open hood and place the pan on the grill grate. Close hood and grill for 15 minutes, flipping halfway through. Grill until the eggs are puffed, browned, and firm in the center. Remove from the grill grate. 8. Slide the frittata out of the pan onto a serving plate. Cut into wedges and serve immediately.

Mexican-style Green Chile-Cheese Corn Bread

Prep Time: 15 minutes | Cook Time: 30 minutes | Serves: 5

Nonstick cooking spray
1 cup all-purpose flour
1 cup yellow cornmeal
¼ cup sugar
2½ teaspoons baking powder
½ teaspoon kosher salt

1 cup whole milk
1 (14.75-ounce) can cream-style corn
4 tablespoons (½ stick) unsalted butter, melted
2 large eggs, beaten
1 (4-ounce) can fire-roasted diced green chiles
½ cup shredded Mexican-style cheese blend

1. To install grill grate, position it flat on top of the heating element so it sits in place, then close hood. Use pellet scoop to pour pellets into smoke box until filled to top. 2. Select GRILL. Select WOODFIRE FLAVOR. Set grill temperature to LO. Set the time to 30 minutes. Select START/STOP to begin preheating. 3. Lightly coat a baking pan with cooking spray. 4. In a medium bowl, whisk the flour, cornmeal, baking powder, sugar, and salt well. 5. In another medium bowl, stir together the milk, corn, melted butter, eggs, green chiles, and cheese until well combined. Pour the wet ingredients into the dry ingredients and gently stir to combine. There should be no signs of flour in the mixture when finished (don't overwork the batter). Transfer the batter to the prepared baking dish. 6. When unit beeps to signify it has preheated and ADD FOOD displays, open hood and place the baking dish on the grill grate. Close hood and grill for 30 minutes, flipping halfway through. Grill until a butter knife inserted into the center of the corn bread comes out clean. 7. Slice the corn bread into squares and serve warm.

Homemade Breakfast Pork Sausage

Prep Time: 50 minutes | Cook Time: 8 minutes | Serves: 8

4 feet medium 1⅓- to 1½-inch diameter) hog casings
2 pounds pork butt, trimmed and cut into 1-inch dice
3 tablespoons finely chopped fresh sage

1 tablespoon kosher salt
2 teaspoons freshly ground black pepper

1. Prepare your casings according to the package directions. Refrigerate a mixing bowl and all the meat grinder and sausage stuffer parts. Freeze the meat uncovered for 30 to 60 minutes. 2. Assemble your grinder according to the manufacturer's directions with the coarse (⅜-inch) die. Place the bowl next to the grinder and grind the meat into the bowl. 3. Add the sage, salt, and pepper. Knead into the meat for at least 5 minutes, then refrigerate. 4. Assemble your stuffer according to the manufacturer's directions. Lubricate the horn with a bit of water and slide the casing onto it. Dampen your work surface. Stuff the meat into the casing, tying off the open ends at the beginning and end. Using a toothpick or cake tester, prick any air bubbles. 5. Twist off the links roughly 4 to 5 inches apart, alternating directions as you twist. 6. Refrigerate overnight, uncovered, on a wire rack set over a sheet pan. 7. To install grill grate, position it flat on top of the heating element so it sits in place, then close hood. Use pellet scoop to pour pellets into smoke box until filled to top. 8. Select GRILL. Select WOODFIRE FLAVOR. Set grill temperature to HI. Set the time to 8 minutes. Select START/STOP to begin preheating. 9. Cut apart the links. When unit beeps to signify it has preheated and ADD FOOD displays, open hood and place the sausage on the grill grate. Close hood and grill for 8 minutes or until an instant-read thermometer inserted in the center registers 160°F. 10. Remove from the grill grate. Let rest for 10 minutes before serving.

Honey Corn Bread

Prep Time: 20 minutes | Cook Time: 1 hour | Serves: 8

½ cup corn oil, plus ½ tablespoon
1 cup yellow cornmeal
1¼ cups all-purpose flour
½ cup granulated sugar
1 tablespoon baking powder
1 teaspoon baking soda

½ teaspoon flaked sea salt
1 cup buttermilk
¼ cup clover honey
3 tablespoons unsalted butter, melted
2 large eggs, lightly beaten
1 cup corn kernels

1. Brush a large baking pan with ½ tablespoon of the corn oil. Set aside. 2. In a medium bowl, whisk together the cornmeal, flour, sugar, baking powder, baking soda, and salt. 3. In a large bowl, whisk together the buttermilk, remaining ½ cup of corn oil, honey, melted butter, and eggs until smooth. 4. Pour the dry ingredients into the wet ingredients and fold to combine. Do not overmix the batter. Pour the batter into the prepared pan and smooth the top. Scatter the corn kernels over the top. 5. To install the grill grate, position it flat on top of the heating element so it sits in place. 6. Place pan on the grill grate, then close the hood. 7. Use the pellet scoop to pour pellets into the smoke box until filled to the top. Select SMOKER. Set grill temperature to 275°F and time to 1 hour. Select START/STOP to begin cooking. Smoke until a toothpick inserted into the thickest part of the corn bread comes out clean.

Grilled Shakshouka

Prep Time: 15 minutes | Cook Time: 40 minutes | Serves: 4

1 tablespoon extra-virgin olive oil
1 medium onion, chopped
3 garlic cloves, chopped
2 medium bell peppers, seeded and chopped
1 large tomato, chopped
2 teaspoons cumin seeds
1 teaspoon ground coriander

½ teaspoon cayenne pepper
Kosher salt
Freshly ground black pepper
1 (15-ounce) can diced tomatoes
4 large eggs
½ cup crumbled feta cheese (optional)
¼ cup chopped fresh mint or flat-leaf parsley

1. To install grill grate, position it flat on top of the heating element so it sits in place, then close hood. Use pellet scoop to pour pellets into smoke box until filled to top. 2. Select GRILL. Select WOODFIRE FLAVOR. Set grill temperature to LO. Set the time to 26 minutes. Select START/STOP to begin preheating. 3. When preheating is complete, pour the oil into a round baking pan that fits your grill and close the hood. Once hot, add the onion, garlic, peppers, chopped tomato, cumin seeds, coriander, and cayenne. Season with salt and pepper and stir to combine. Close the hood and cook, stirring once or twice, for 26 minutes or until softened. 4. Stir in the diced tomatoes with their juice. Close the hood and cook for 9 to 12 minutes or until thickened slightly. 5. Form four wells in the sauce and add one egg to each well. Close the hood and cook for 4 to 6 minutes or until the whites have set but the yolks are still runny. 6. Remove from the grill, sprinkle with the feta (if using) and mint, and serve immediately.

Butternut Squash-Bacon Bread Pudding

Prep Time: 15 minutes | Cook Time: 2 hours | Serves: 8

1-pound bacon slices, cut into ½-inch pieces
6 large eggs, lightly beaten
2 cups heavy (whipping) cream
3 thyme sprigs, leaves stripped and finely chopped
Flaked sea salt
Freshly ground black pepper

1 large butternut squash, peeled, halved lengthwise, seeded, and diced
3 leeks, white parts only, quartered lengthwise and thinly sliced
1 baguette loaf, diced
2 cups finely grated Parmesan cheese

1. To install the grill grate, position it flat on top of the heating element so it sits in place. 2. Place the bacon in a baking pan and place the pan on the grill grate, then close the hood. 3. Use the pellet scoop to pour pellets into the smoke box until filled to the top. Select SMOKER. Set grill temperature to 275°F and time to 30 minutes. Select START/STOP to begin cooking. 4. Smoke the bacon for 30 minutes, or until golden brown, tossing occasionally. Remove the bacon to a plate, set aside. Spoon off and discard the excess fat. 5. In a large bowl, combine the eggs, heavy cream, and thyme leaves. Season with salt and pepper. Whisk to combine. Set aside. 6. Add the butternut squash and leeks to the pan. Season with salt and pepper. Smoke for 30 minutes. Then add the smoked bacon. 7. Add the bread cubes to the pan and gently fold them into the squash and leeks. 8. Pour the egg mixture evenly over the pan ingredients. Top with the Parmesan cheese and season with salt and pepper (keep in mind the Parmesan is quite salty). Smoke for 1 hour, or until golden brown and fully set. Let cool slightly before serving.

Garlic-Butter Bread

Prep Time: 15 minutes | Cook Time: 30 minutes | Serves: 8

2 (11-ounce) tubes French bread dough
1 stick butter, melted
2 tablespoons garlic paste

Kosher salt
Freshly ground black pepper

1. To install the grill grate, position it flat on top of the heating element so it sits in place. 2. Select the BAKE function. Adjust the temperature to 350°F and time to 30 minutes. Select START/STOP to begin preheating. 3. Slice the bread dough into 1-inch segments. In a small bowl, combine the butter, garlic paste, along with a pinch of salt and pepper. 4. Dip each bread piece into the garlic butter and place in a baking pan. Pour any remaining garlic butter over top. 5. When preheating is complete, open the hood and place the baking pan on the grate. Once the hood is closed, cooking will begin and the timer will start counting down.

Chapter 2 Vegetables and Sides Recipes

Lemony Asparagus with Almonds

Prep Time: 10 minutes | Cook Time: 20-30 minutes | Serves: 4

1 tablespoon extra-virgin olive oil
1 tablespoon unsalted butter
1-pound fresh asparagus, woody ends trimmed
4 shallots, trimmed and quartered

Flaked sea salt
Freshly ground black pepper
1 lemon, halved and seeded, for serving
1 cup sliced almonds

1. Melt the butter in your microwave. Then add the butter and olive oil to the baking pan. 2. Add the asparagus and shallots to the pan. Season with salt and pepper and toss to coat in the oil and butter and seasoning. Place the lemon halves in the pan, cut-side down. 3. To install the grill grate, position it flat on top of the heating element so it sits in place. 4. Place the baking pan on the grill grate lengthwise, then close the hood. 5. Use the pellet scoop to pour pellets into the smoke box until filled to the top. Select SMOKER. Set grill temperature to 275°F and time to 20 minutes. Select START/STOP to begin cooking, tossing once during smoking. 6. To serve, add a squeeze or two from the charred lemons and top with the almonds.

Easy Smoked Butternut Squash

Prep Time: 15 minutes | Cook Time: 1 hour | Serves: 4

2 butternut squash
3 tablespoons olive oil

1½ teaspoons coarse salt

1. Cut off the top inch or so of each squash, then slice them in half lengthwise. Leave the seeds intact. Brush the flesh with olive oil, and season with salt. 2. To install the grill grate, position it flat on top of the heating element so it sits in place. 3. Place the butternut squash on the grill grate, cut-side up on the grill grate, then close the hood. 4. Use the pellet scoop to pour pellets into the smoke box until filled to the top. Select SMOKER. Set grill temperature to 275°F and time to 1 hour. Select START/STOP to begin cooking. The squash should be tender when done. 5. Remove and let it cool for at least 15 to 20 minutes before handling. Discard the seeds, scoop out the flesh, and use or store as needed.

BBQ Sauce Smoked Beans

Prep Time: 10 minutes | Cook Time: 1½ hours | Serves: 4

3 (28-ounce) cans baked beans
¾ cup barbecue sauce of choice
½ cup yellow mustard

½ cup brown sugar
2 tablespoons Worcestershire sauce

1. To install the grill grate, position it flat on top of the heating element so it sits in place. 2. Place the beans into a baking pan. Add the barbecue sauce, mustard, brown sugar, and Worcestershire sauce. Stir until combined. 3. Place the pan on the grill grate, then close the hood. 4. Use the pellet scoop to pour pellets into the smoke box until filled to the top. Select SMOKER. Set grill temperature to 250°F and time to 1½ hours. Select START/STOP to begin cooking, stirring a few times throughout.

Tasty Jerk-Marinated Tofu

Prep Time: 30 minutes | Cook Time: 15 minutes | Serves: 2

1 (12-ounce) block extra-firm tofu
⅓ cup jerk marinade

2 tablespoons soy sauce

1. Press the tofu for 30 minutes using a heavy weight (such as a cast iron skillet). Pat dry and transfer to a shallow dish. Pour in the marinade and turn the tofu over to coat; marinate for 30 minutes at room temperature. 2. To install grill grate, position it flat on top of the heating element so it sits in place, then close hood. Use pellet scoop to pour pellets into smoke box until filled to top. 3. Select GRILL. Select WOODFIRE FLAVOR. Set grill temperature to HI. Set the time to 15 minutes. Select START/STOP to begin preheating. 4. When unit beeps to signify it has preheated and ADD FOOD displays, open hood and place the tofu on the grill grate. Close hood and grill for 15 minutes. Cook until the marinade has caramelized around the edges and the tofu is heated through. Transfer to a plate. 5. Cut into ¼-inch-thick slices, drizzle with the soy sauce, and serve immediately.

Honey-Bourbon Glazed Carrots

Prep Time: 10 minutes | Cook Time: 35 minutes | Serves: 6

2 pounds whole carrots (preferably with tops)
1 teaspoon kosher salt
For the Glaze:
3 tablespoons cold unsalted butter
3 tablespoons honey

1 teaspoon freshly ground black pepper
1 teaspoon fresh thyme leaves

3 tablespoons bourbon

1. In a small saucepan on the stovetop over medium-low heat, melt the butter. Add the honey and bourbon and stir until they are fully incorporated. Simmer the glaze for 5 minutes, until it thickens. Remove it from the heat. 2. If your carrots have tops, cut them down to about 1 inch. If your carrots are really large, you may need to halve them lengthwise, so they cook evenly. 3. Brush the carrots with the glaze, season them with the salt and pepper. 4. To install grill grate, position it flat on top of the heating element so it sits in place, then close hood. Use pellet scoop to pour pellets into smoke box until filled to top. 5. Select GRILL. Select WOODFIRE FLAVOR. Set grill temperature to LO. Set the time to 25 minutes. Select START/STOP to begin preheating. 6. When unit beeps to signify it has preheated and ADD FOOD displays, open hood and place the carrots on the grill grate. Close hood and grill for 25 minutes, turning them with a pair of long-handled tongs and brushing them with more glaze every 5 minutes, until they are slightly charred all over and fork-tender. 7. Remove the carrots from the grill grate. Drizzle the carrots with the remaining glaze and sprinkle with the thyme leaves before serving.

Balsamic Brussels Sprouts & Bacon

Prep Time: 15 minutes | Cook Time: 55 minutes | Serves: 4

6 thick-cut bacon slices
1 small yellow onion, thinly sliced
2 garlic cloves, finely chopped
1½ pounds Brussels sprouts, washed, stems and excess leaves removed

1 tablespoon olive oil
½ teaspoon salt
½ teaspoon freshly ground black pepper
2 tablespoons balsamic vinegar

1. Cook the bacon in a large skillet over medium heat until the fat renders, about 7 minutes. Once cooked, remove the bacon and use 3 to 4 tablespoons of the bacon fat to sauté the onion. After 2 minutes, stir in the garlic. Cook for 1 minute more, then remove from heat. 2. Place the Brussels sprouts in a baking pan with the onion and garlic. 3. Chop the bacon into small pieces and add to the Brussels sprouts. Add the olive oil, salt, and pepper to the pan and toss to combine. 4. To install the grill grate, position it flat on top of the heating element so it sits in place. 5. Select the ROAST function. Adjust the temperature to 250°F and time to 45 minutes. Select START/STOP to begin preheating. 6. When preheating is complete, open the hood and place the baking pan on the grill grate. Once the hood is closed, cooking will begin and the timer will begin counting down. 7. When cook time reaches zero, the grill will beep and DONE will appear on the display. Remove food from grill grate. Drizzle with balsamic vinegar, then serve.

Cheese Jalapeño Corn Bread

Prep Time: 10 minutes | Cook Time: 25 minutes | Serves: 8

1 cup cornmeal
1 cup all-purpose flour
¼ cup sugar
2 teaspoons baking powder
½ teaspoon baking soda
Pinch Kosher salt

1½ cups buttermilk
2 eggs
5 tablespoons melted butter, divided
2 jalapeño peppers (minced)
1 cup shredded cheddar cheese

1. In a large bowl, whisk together the cornmeal, flour, sugar, baking powder, baking soda, and salt to combine. 2. Add the buttermilk, eggs, and 3 tablespoons of butter to the dry ingredients. Stir until evenly combined. 3. Gently fold in the jalapeños and shredded cheese.4. Pour the remaining 2 tablespoons of butter in the baking pan and spread evenly. Pour the corn bread batter into the pan. 5. To install the grill grate, position it flat on top of the heating element so it sits in place. 6. Select the BAKE function. Adjust the temperature to 400°F and time to 25 minutes. Select START/STOP to begin preheating. 7. When preheating is complete, open the hood and place the baking pan on the grate. Once the hood is closed, cooking will begin and the timer will start counting down. 8. When cook time reaches zero, the grill will beep and DONE will appear on the display. Remove food from grill grate.

Caramelized Onions

Prep Time: 15 minutes | Cook Time: 3 hours | Serves: 6

4 yellow onions
4 tablespoons butter
3 tablespoons brown sugar

3 tablespoons balsamic vinegar
Kosher salt
Freshly ground black pepper

1. Slice the onions thinly and arrange them in a baking pan. Divide the butter into smaller pieces and scatter them over the onions. Then, add the brown sugar, balsamic vinegar, and a pinch of salt and pepper to the onions. 2. To install the grill grate, position it flat on top of the heating element so it sits in place. 3. Place ribs on the grill grate lengthwise, then close the hood. 4. Use the pellet scoop to pour pellets into the smoke box until filled to the top. Select SMOKER. Set grill temperature to 275°F and time to 3 hours. Select START/STOP to begin cooking, stirring the onions every half hour.

Grilled Cajun Corn on the Cob

Prep Time: 5 minutes | Cook Time: 12 minutes | Serves: 6

2 tablespoons melted butter
½ tablespoon garlic paste
1 tablespoon Cajun seasoning, divided

Kosher salt
Freshly ground black pepper
6 ears corn on the cob, shucked

1. To install grill grate, position it flat on top of the heating element so it sits in place, then close hood. Use pellet scoop to pour pellets into smoke box until filled to top. 2. Select GRILL. Select WOODFIRE FLAVOR. Set grill temperature to LO. Set the time to 12 minutes. Select START/STOP to begin preheating. 3. In a bowl, combine the garlic paste, butter, and 1½ teaspoons of Cajun seasoning. 4. Brush the Cajun garlic butter on all sides of the corn and sprinkle with the remaining 1½ teaspoons of Cajun seasoning and a pinch each of salt and pepper. 5. When unit beeps to signify it has preheated and ADD FOOD displays, open hood and place the corn on the grill grate. Close hood and grill for 12 minutes, turning a few times throughout.

Homemade Holiday Stuffing

Prep Time: 15 minutes | Cook Time: 1 hour 20 minutes | Serves: 4

2 tablespoons olive oil
12 ounces chicken-apple sausage, casings removed
1 small yellow onion, chopped
2 large celery stalks, chopped
2 garlic cloves, minced
16 ounces stuffing cubes, homemade or prepackaged
2 medium sweet apples, peeled, cored, and chopped

2 large eggs
3 cups vegetable broth
½ teaspoon dried sage
½ teaspoon salt
½ teaspoon dried rosemary
½ teaspoon red pepper flakes (optional)
3 tablespoons melted butter

1. Heat the olive oil in a large skillet over medium heat. Add the sausage and sauté for 3 to 4 minutes. Add the onion, celery, and garlic and cook for 2 to 3 minutes, until the vegetables start to become tender. Stir in the stuffing cubes and apples. Remove from heat and set aside. 2. In a large bowl, whisk together the eggs, vegetable broth, sage, salt, rosemary, and red pepper flakes (if using). Add the contents of the skillet to the egg mixture and gently fold to combine. Place the stuffing in a baking pan and drizzle with the melted butter. 3. To install the grill grate, position it flat on top of the heating element so it sits in place. 4. Place the baking pan on the grill grate lengthwise, then close the hood. 5. Use the pellet scoop to pour pellets into the smoke box until filled to the top. Select SMOKER. Set grill temperature to 225°F and time to 1 hour 20 minutes. Select START/STOP to begin cooking. Cook until the stuffing is browned and slightly crispy on top. 6. Remove and serve.

Grilled Chimichurri Eggplant

Prep Time: 15 minutes | Cook Time: 6 minutes | Serves: 4

2 Italian eggplants
3 tablespoons olive oil

1 batch Argentinian-Style Chimichurri

1. Prepare the eggplant. Peel each eggplant and cut lengthwise into ½-inch-thick slices. Brush with olive oil. 2. To install grill grate, position it flat on top of the heating element so it sits in place, then close hood. Use pellet scoop to pour pellets into smoke box until filled to top. 3. Select GRILL. Select WOODFIRE FLAVOR. Set grill temperature to LO. Set the time to 6 minutes. Select START/STOP to begin preheating. 4. When unit beeps to signify it has preheated and ADD FOOD displays, open hood and oil the grill grate. Place the eggplant slices on the grill grate. Close hood and grill for 6 minutes, turning frequently and basting with chimichurri sauce, until the eggplant is well browned and soft, but still slightly firm. 5. Remove from the grill grate and serve immediately with more chimichurri on the side, if desired.

Simple Grilled Asparagus with Sauce Gribiche

Prep Time: 10 minutes | Cook Time: 6 minutes | Serves: 8

2 bunches fresh asparagus (thicker is better; about 2 pounds), woody ends snapped off where they naturally break—you'll know
Sauce Gribiche:
1 cup good-quality mayonnaise
3 large hard-boiled eggs, peeled and finely chopped
Juice of ½ lemon
2 tablespoons chopped shallot
1 tablespoon capers, drained and rinsed

Garlic-infused oil or olive oil as needed
Kosher salt and freshly ground black pepper

1 tablespoon chopped cornichons (you can substitute dill pickles)
1 tablespoon chopped fresh flat-leaf parsley
1 tablespoon chopped fresh chives
1 teaspoon chopped fresh dill
1 teaspoon Dijon mustard

1. In a medium bowl, whisk the sauce Gribiche ingredients together. Refrigerate in an airtight container for at least 3 hours (overnight is even better); it will keep 3 to 4 days. 2. Arrange the asparagus on a rimmed baking sheet. Drizzle with oil and season to taste with salt and pepper. Roll the asparagus around in the oil to coat evenly. 3. To install grill grate, position it flat on top of the heating element so it sits in place, then close hood. Use pellet scoop to pour pellets into smoke box until filled to top. 4. Select GRILL. Select WOODFIRE FLAVOR. Set grill temperature to HI. Set the time to 6 minutes. Select START/STOP to begin preheating. 5. When unit beeps to signify it has preheated and ADD FOOD displays, open hood and place the asparagus on the grill grate. Close hood and grill for 6 minutes, flipping halfway through, rolling the asparagus with a spatula, much like you would with hot dogs. When they pick up some char, they are done. You want the asparagus to be slightly crisp, so taste one to check on doneness. 6. Transfer the asparagus to a platter and serve hot off the grill or at room temperature with the sauce Gribiche on the side.

Grilled Vegetable Kebabs

Prep Time: 20 minutes | Cook Time: 12 minutes | Serves: 4

12 pearl onions, peeled
½ cup olive oil, divided
¼ cup red wine vinegar
1 tablespoon dried oregano
1 tablespoon dried parsley
1 teaspoon dried thyme

1 teaspoon salt
½ teaspoon red pepper flakes
1 red bell pepper, cut into 1-inch cubes
12 small mushrooms, stemmed
2 zucchinis, cut in 1-inch rounds
2 garlic cloves, minced

1. Prepare the vegetables. Put the onions in a microwave-safe dish and drizzle with 1 tablespoon of olive oil. Microwave on high power for 2 minutes until slightly tender. 2. Marinate. In a large bowl, whisk the remaining 7 tablespoons of olive oil, the vinegar, oregano, parsley, thyme, salt, and red pepper flakes until well mixed. Add the onions, red bell pepper, mushrooms, zucchini, and garlic. Toss to coat and combine. Let marinate at room temperature for at least 30 minutes. 3. Make the kebabs. Remove the vegetables from the marinade and place them on about 4 skewers until the skewers are almost full. Discard the marinade. 4. To install grill grate, position it flat on top of the heating element so it sits in place, then close hood. Use pellet scoop to pour pellets into smoke box until filled to top. 5. Select GRILL. Select WOODFIRE FLAVOR. Set grill temperature to LO. Set the time to 12 minutes. Select START/STOP to begin preheating. 6. When unit beeps to signify it has preheated and ADD FOOD displays, open hood and oil the grill grate. Place the kebabs on the grill grate. Close hood and grill for 12 minutes, turning every 2 minutes, until the vegetables are tender and have black grill marks around the edges. 7. Rest. Let rest for 5 minutes, then serve immediately.

Smoked Chantilly Potatoes

Prep Time: 20 minutes | Cook Time: 1 hour | Serves: 4

4 medium russet potatoes, peeled and cut into 1-inch cubes
1 cup heavy cream
½ cup butter, melted
1 cup shredded Gouda cheese

1 teaspoon salt
½ teaspoon freshly ground black pepper
¼ teaspoon garlic powder
½ cup shredded Parmesan cheese

1. Bring a large pot of water to a boil over high heat. Add the potatoes and boil until tender, about 20 minutes. Drain and mash the potatoes with a fork. 2. Place the cooked potatoes in a large bowl. Add the cream, melted butter, Gouda, salt, black pepper, and garlic powder. Taste and adjust salt as needed. 3. Scoop the mixture into a baking pan and top with the Parmesan cheese. 4. To install the grill grate, position it flat on top of the heating element so it sits in place. 5. Place the baking pan on the grill grate lengthwise, then close the hood. 6. Use the pellet scoop to pour pellets into the smoke box until filled to the top. Select SMOKER. Set grill temperature to 275°F and time to 40 minutes. Select START/STOP to begin cooking. 7. The cheese will have melted and the potatoes will appear golden brown around the edges when done. 8. Remove and serve immediately.

Herb-Smoked Potatoes with Goose Fat

Prep Time: 15 minutes | Cook Time: 2 hours 45 minutes | Serves: 8

Coarse sea salt
5 pounds russet potatoes, scrubbed with skins left on
3 fresh bay leaves
8 ounces goose (or duck) fat
12 garlic cloves, unpeeled

Flaked sea salt
Freshly ground black pepper
3 thyme sprigs, leaves stripped and finely chopped
3 rosemary sprigs, leaves stripped

1. Fill a large stockpot with cold water until it's three-fourths full. Generously season the water with coarse sea salt and add the potatoes and bay leaves. Place the pot over high heat and bring the water to a boil. Reduce the heat to medium and cook for about 45 minutes, or until the potatoes are tender. Remove the potatoes from the water and let them cool slightly. 2. Using a paring knife, gently peel the potatoes. Quarter them lengthwise. 3. To install the grill grate, position it flat on top of the heating element so it sits in place. 4. Place a baking pan on the grill grate, add the goose fat to melt. Arrange the potatoes and garlic on the pan, season with flaked sea salt and pepper, and toss to coat. 5. Use the pellet scoop to pour pellets into the smoke box until filled to the top. Select SMOKER. Set grill temperature to 275°F and time to 1 hour. Select START/STOP to begin cooking. 6. Remove the baking pan from the smoker and gently turn the potatoes. 7. Add the thyme and rosemary. Return the pan to the smoker and smoke for 1 hour more, until the potatoes are golden brown, turning 2 or 3 times. Remove and discard the herbs. Finish with flaked sea salt.

Roasted Sweet Potato Slices

Prep Time: 20 minutes | Cook Time: 23 minutes | Serves: 4

4 sweet potatoes
¼ cup canola oil
1 teaspoon salt

1 teaspoon garlic powder
1 teaspoon ground ginger
1 teaspoon dried mustard

1. Prepare the sweet potatoes. Wash the sweet potatoes well and dry with a paper towel. Cut each sweet potato on the diagonal into ½-inch-thick slices. Put the sweet potato slices in a large microwave-safe bowl and pour the canola oil over them. Mix until coated. Microwave on high power for 3 to 4 minutes until tender, but not mushy. Let cool slightly. 2. Season. In a small bowl, stir together the salt, garlic powder, ginger, and dried mustard. Sprinkle the seasoning over the sweet potatoes and toss until well coated. Cover and let sit in the seasoning at room temperature for 30 minutes. 3. To install the grill grate, position it flat on top of the heating element so it sits in place. 4. Select the ROAST function. Adjust the temperature to 380°F and time to 20 minutes. Select START/STOP to begin preheating. 5. When preheating is complete, open the hood and place the sweet potatoes on the grill grate. Once the hood is closed, cooking will begin and the timer will begin counting down, turning frequently. Roast until the sweet potatoes are soft. Serve immediately.

Smoked Cheesy Hash Brown Potatoes

Prep Time: 15 minutes | Cook Time: 1 hour 20 minutes | Serves: 6

2 tablespoons olive oil
1 small yellow onion, diced
2 garlic cloves, minced
3 cups corn flake cereal, crushed
½ cup melted butter, divided
1 (30-ounce) bag frozen hash browns
1 (15-ounce) can cream of mushroom soup

1 cup shredded sharp cheddar cheese
1 cup sour cream
⅓ cup shredded Parmesan cheese
¼ cup mayonnaise
1 teaspoon salt
½ teaspoon freshly ground black pepper
1 (4-ounce) can diced mild green chiles (optional)

1. Heat the oil in a large saucepan over medium heat. Add the onion and cook for 3 minutes, stirring often. Add the garlic and cook for 1 minute. Remove from the heat. 2. Prepare the topping by combining the crushed corn flake cereal with ¼ cup of melted butter in a large bowl. 3. In a separate bowl, combine the frozen hash browns with the remaining ¼ cup of melted butter, along with the cream of mushroom soup, sharp cheddar, sour cream, Parmesan, mayonnaise, salt, pepper, and chiles (if using). Fold to combine. Place the hash brown mixture into a baking pan and top with the corn flake mixture. 4. To install the grill grate, position it flat on top of the heating element so it sits in place. 5. Place the pan on the grill grate, then close the hood. 6. Use the pellet scoop to pour pellets into the smoke box until filled to the top. Select SMOKER. Set grill temperature to 225°F and time to 1 hour and 15 minutes. Select START/STOP to begin cooking. 7. Once cooked, remove the pan from the smoker and serve immediately.

Smoked Heirloom Carrots & Jalapeño

Prep Time: 15 minutes | Cook Time: 1 hour | Serves: 8

1 tablespoon extra-virgin olive oil
1 tablespoon unsalted butter
24 rainbow heirloom carrots, scrubbed, trimmed, and quartered lengthwise
3 jalapeño peppers, trimmed, seeded, and cut into rings

3 rosemary sprigs, plus extra rosemary leaves for garnish
Flaked sea salt
Freshly ground black pepper
Grated zest of 1 lemon
3 tablespoons wildflower honey

1. In a skillet over medium heat, pour in the olive oil and add the butter to melt. 2. Add the carrots, jalapeños, and rosemary to the skillet. Season with salt and pepper and toss to coat. Spread the vegetables into an even layer in a baking pan. 3. To install the grill grate, position it flat on top of the heating element so it sits in place. 4. Place the pan on the grill grate, then close the hood. 5. Use the pellet scoop to pour pellets into the smoke box until filled to the top. Select SMOKER. Set grill temperature to 250°F and time to 1 hour. Select START/STOP to begin cooking. Smoke until the vegetables are tender, caramelized, and golden brown, turning once during smoking. Remove the pan from the smoker. Remove and discard the rosemary sprigs. 6. To serve, sprinkle with lemon zest, drizzle with honey, and garnish with fresh rosemary leaves.

Spicy Garlic Black Beans

Prep Time: 20 minutes | Cook Time: 2 hours | Serves: 8

1 tablespoon extra-virgin olive oil
1 tablespoon unsalted butter
1 yellow onion, diced
1 jalapeño pepper, trimmed, seeded, diced, plus more for additional heat
3 garlic cloves, minced

Flaked sea salt
Freshly ground black pepper
6 cups black turtle beans
3 fresh bay leaves
2 cups chicken (or vegetable) stock

1. Melt the butter in your microwave and pour into a baking pan. Then add the olive oil to the pan. 2. Add the onion, jalapeño, and garlic to the pan. Season with salt and pepper and toss to coat with the oil and butter. 3. To install the grill grate, position it flat on top of the heating element so it sits in place. 4. Place the pan on the grill grate, then close the hood. 5. Use the pellet scoop to pour pellets into the smoke box until filled to the top. Select SMOKER. Set grill temperature to 250°F and time to 30 minutes. Select START/STOP to begin cooking. 6. Using a heatproof spatula, stir in the beans, bay leaves, and chicken stock. Smoke for 90 minutes, or until soft. Taste and season with more jalapeño, salt, and pepper, as needed.

Smoked Potatoes with Shallots

Prep Time: 20 minutes | Cook Time: 1 hour 20 minutes | Serves: 8

Coarse sea salt
2 pounds fingerling potatoes, rinsed
2 fresh bay leaves
2 tablespoons extra-virgin olive oil
2 tablespoons unsalted butter

8 shallots, trimmed and quartered lengthwise
Flaked sea salt
Freshly ground black pepper
2 parsley sprigs, leaves stripped and minced

1. Fill a large stockpot with cold water until it's three-fourths full. Generously season the water with coarse sea salt and add the potatoes and bay leaves. Place the pot over high heat and bring the water to a boil. Reduce the heat to medium and cook for about 30 minutes, or until the potatoes are tender. Remove the potatoes from the water and let them cool slightly. Halve the potatoes. 2. Melt the butter in your microwave and pour into a baking pan. Then add the olive oil to the pan. 3. Add the potatoes and shallots to the pan. Season with salt and pepper and toss to coat. 4. To install the grill grate, position it flat on top of the heating element so it sits in place. 5. Place the pan on the grill grate, then close the hood. 6. Use the pellet scoop to pour pellets into the smoke box until filled to the top. Select SMOKER. Set grill temperature to 250°F and time to 50 minutes. Select START/STOP to begin cooking. Cook until golden brown, tossing occasionally. 7. Top with fresh parsley and flaked sea salt to taste.

Homemade Pico De Gallo

Prep Time: 15 minutes | Cook Time: 0 minutes | Serves: 8

12 Roma tomatoes, stemmed, quartered, and diced
1 red onion, diced
1 bunch fresh cilantro, leaves stripped and finely chopped
1 jalapeño pepper, trimmed, seeded, and finely chopped

Grated zest of 3 limes, plus juice of 3 limes
Flaked sea salt
Freshly ground black pepper
3 canned chipotle peppers in adobo sauce, finely chopped

1. In a large bowl, stir together the tomatoes, onion, cilantro, jalapeño, lime zest, and lime juice. Taste and season with salt and pepper. 2. Stir in the chipotle peppers a little bit at a time, tasting as you go, until your desired spice level is reached.

Mint Beet Salad

Prep Time: 15 minutes | Cook Time: 40 minutes | Serves: 4

6 medium beets, scrubbed
1 tablespoon vegetable oil
1 cup fresh mint leaves, chopped
¼ cup pepitas
1 tablespoon extra-virgin olive oil

Juice of ¼ lemon
Kosher salt
Freshly ground black pepper
¼ cup crumbled goat cheese

1. In a large bowl, toss the beets with the vegetable oil to coat. Wrap each in aluminum foil. 2. To install the grill grate, position it flat on top of the heating element so it sits in place. 3. Select the ROAST function. Adjust the temperature to 475°F and time to 40 minutes. Select START/ STOP to begin preheating. 4. When preheating is complete, open the hood and place the beets on the grill grate. Once the hood is closed, cooking will begin and the timer will begin counting down. 5. When cook time reaches zero, the grill will beep and DONE will appear on the display. Remove food from grill grate. 6. Once cool enough to handle, peel the beets, then cut into ¼-inch dice. Transfer to a large bowl. 7. Toss with the mint, pepitas, oil, and lemon juice. Season with salt and pepper. Top with the goat cheese. Serve immediately or at room temperature.

Cheese Corn Pudding

Prep Time: 20 minutes | Cook Time: 50 minutes | Serves: 6

2 eggs
1 (12-ounce) can evaporated milk
2½ tablespoons all-purpose flour
2 tablespoons melted butter
1½ cups corn kernels (about 4 medium ears)
1 (15-ounce) can creamed corn

1 cup shredded cheddar cheese
½ cup shredded pepper jack cheese
2 teaspoons white sugar
1 teaspoon salt
½ teaspoon freshly ground black pepper
1 tablespoon vegetable oil

1. In a large bowl, whisk together the eggs, evaporated milk, flour, and melted butter until well combined. Add the corn kernels, creamed corn, cheddar, pepper jack, sugar, salt, and black pepper. Stir to combine. 2. Grease a baking pan with the vegetable oil and pour the corn mixture into it. 3. To install the grill grate, position it flat on top of the heating element so it sits in place. 4. Place the pan on the grill grate, then close the hood. 5. Use the pellet scoop to pour pellets into the smoke box until filled to the top. Select SMOKER. Set grill temperature to 300°F and time to 50 minutes. Select START/STOP to begin cooking. 6. After 50 minutes, check to see if the center has set. If it is still soft, cook for an additional 10 to 15 minutes. The sides should be golden brown and the center slightly firm. Remove from the smoker and let stand for 10 minutes before serving.

Grilled Garlic Polenta

Prep Time: 1 hour 30 minutes | Cook Time: 23 minutes | Serves: 4

3 cups chicken stock
1 teaspoon salt
1 cup polenta
4 tablespoons (½ stick) butter

3 tablespoons olive oil
2 tablespoons paprika
1 tablespoon garlic powder

1. Prepare the polenta. Coat a baking dish with nonstick cooking spray and set aside. In a medium saucepan over high heat, combine the chicken stock and salt and bring to a boil. Whisk in the polenta until dissolved. Cover the pan and simmer on low heat for 20 to 30 minutes, until the polenta is well cooked. It will have a thick consistency and all the water should be absorbed. Stir in the butter and olive oil. Transfer the polenta to the prepared baking dish. Cover and refrigerate for 1 to 24 hours. 2. Season. Sprinkle the paprika and garlic powder over the polenta. Cut the polenta into 2-inch squares and remove them from the baking dish. 3. To install grill grate, position it flat on top of the heating element so it sits in place, then close hood. Use pellet scoop to pour pellets into smoke box until filled to top. 4. Select GRILL. Select WOODFIRE FLAVOR. Set grill temperature to LO. Set the time to 3 minutes. Select START/STOP to begin preheating. 5. When unit beeps to signify it has preheated and ADD FOOD displays, open hood and oil the grill grate. Place the polenta on the grill grate. Close hood and grill for 3 minutes, flipping halfway through. Grill until the grill marks are present. Remove from the grill grate and serve immediately.

Grilled Corn Ears

Prep Time: 5 minutes | Cook Time: 20 minutes | Serves: 4

4 ears corn, husked
2 teaspoons vegetable oil
Kosher salt
4 ounces cotija or feta cheese, crumbled
2 tablespoons unsalted butter

¼ cup crema or sour cream
Chili powder, for dusting
Your favorite hot sauce, for drizzling
Lime wedges, for serving

1. Rub the corn with the oil. Season with salt. 2. To install grill grate, position it flat on top of the heating element so it sits in place, then close hood. Use pellet scoop to pour pellets into smoke box until filled to top. 3. Select GRILL. Select WOODFIRE FLAVOR. Set grill temperature to HI. Set the time to 20 minutes. Select START/STOP to begin preheating. 4. When unit beeps to signify it has preheated and ADD FOOD displays, open hood and place the corn on the grill grate. Close hood and grill for 20 minutes, turning one-quarter turn every 5 to 6 minutes, until tender and charred. Transfer to a plate. 5. Put the cheese on another plate. Once the corn is cool enough to handle, coat with the butter and crema, then roll each cob in the cheese. Dust with chili powder, and drizzle with your favorite hot sauce. Serve immediately with lime wedges on the side.

Savory Bacon with Brussels Sprouts

Prep Time: 15 minutes | Cook Time: 2 hours | Serves: 8

1 tablespoon extra-virgin olive oil
1 tablespoon unsalted butter
1-pound pancetta, cut into ½-inch pieces
4 shallots, trimmed and finely sliced

2 pounds Brussels sprouts, trimmed and halved
Flaked sea salt
Freshly ground black pepper

1. Melt the butter in your microwave and pour into a baking pan. Then add the olive oil to the pan. 2. Add the pancetta and shallots to the pan. 3. To install the grill grate, position it flat on top of the heating element so it sits in place. 4. Place the pan on the grill grate, then close the hood. 5. Use the pellet scoop to pour pellets into the smoke box until filled to the top. Select SMOKER. Set grill temperature to 275°F and time to 1 hour. Select START/STOP to begin cooking. Smoke until golden brown, tossing occasionally. 6. Add the Brussels sprouts to the pan and season with salt and pepper. Smoke for 1 hour, or until golden brown. Cool slightly before serving.

Refreshing Cabbage Slaw

Prep Time: 15 minutes | Cook Time: 0 minutes | Serves: 8

6 tablespoons apple cider vinegar
2 tablespoons wildflower honey
2 tablespoons extra-virgin olive oil
2 tablespoons mayonnaise
1 tablespoon sriracha
1 tablespoon Dijon mustard
1 tablespoon celery seed

8 cups finely shredded Savoy cabbage
2 Fuji apples, cored and cut into matchsticks
2 scallions, trimmed and thinly sliced on an angle
Grated zest of 1 lemon, plus juice of 1 lemon
Flaked sea salt
Freshly ground black pepper

1. In a large bowl, whisk together the vinegar, honey, olive oil, mayonnaise, sriracha, mustard, and celery seed until smooth and combined. 2. Add the cabbage, apples, scallions, lemon zest, and lemon juice. Toss to coat well in the dressing. 3. Cover with plastic wrap and refrigerate for 1 hour. Toss again before serving. Season with salt and pepper to taste.

Grilled Zucchini with Basil & Orange Zest

Prep Time: 5 minutes | Cook Time: 12 minutes | Serves: 6

6 medium zucchini (about 3½ pounds), trimmed and halved lengthwise
2 teaspoons vegetable oil
Kosher salt

Grated zest of 1 orange
15 to 20 fresh basil leaves, torn
Extra-virgin olive oil, for serving
Freshly ground black pepper

1. In a large bowl, toss the zucchini with the oil. Season with salt. 2. To install grill grate, position it flat on top of the heating element so it sits in place, then close hood. Use pellet scoop to pour pellets into smoke box until filled to top. 3. Select GRILL. Select WOODFIRE FLAVOR. Set grill temperature to HI. Set the time to 12 minutes. Select START/STOP to begin preheating. 4. When unit beeps to signify it has preheated and ADD FOOD displays, open hood and place the zucchini on the grill grate. Close hood and grill for 12 minutes, flipping halfway through. Cook until tender and grill marks appear. Transfer to a serving dish. 5. Sprinkle with the orange zest and basil, then drizzle with olive oil. Season with pepper. Serve immediately.

Roasted Carrots Salad

Prep Time: 20 minutes | Cook Time: 15 minutes | Serves: 4

8 medium carrots (about 1½ pounds), peeled
1 teaspoon vegetable oil
Kosher salt
1 tablespoon honey
Juice of ¼ lemon

1 tablespoon extra-virgin olive oil
1 teaspoon cumin seeds, toasted
1 tablespoon sesame seeds, toasted
10 fresh cilantro sprigs
Freshly ground black pepper

1. To install the grill grate, position it flat on top of the heating element so it sits in place. 2. Select the ROAST function. Adjust the temperature to 450°F and time to 15 minutes. Select START/STOP to begin preheating. 3. On a baking sheet, toss the carrots with the vegetable oil to coat. Season with salt; toss again. 4. When preheating is complete, open the hood and place the carrots on the grill grate. Once the hood is closed, cooking will begin and the timer will begin counting down. 5. When cook time reaches zero, the grill will beep and DONE will appear on the display. 6. Transfer to a plate and refrigerate. 7. Once just cool enough to handle, cut the carrots into 1-inch pieces on an angle. Transfer to a bowl. 8. Toss with the honey, lemon juice, olive oil, cumin and sesame seeds, and cilantro. Season with salt and pepper. Serve at room temperature or chilled.

Chapter 3 Poultry Recipes

Roasted Garlic Turkey

Prep Time: 10 minutes | Cook Time: 3 hours | Serves: 12

1 (12- to 14-pound) turkey, giblets removed, rinsed, and patted dry
2 tablespoons kosher salt
1 tablespoon freshly ground black pepper
1 tablespoon dried herbes de Provence
1 tablespoon grated lemon zest

1 teaspoon dried sage
1 onion, quartered
1 rib celery, cut into chunks
6 cloves garlic, mashed with the back of your knife
½ cup (1 stick) unsalted butter, melted

1. Two days before you plan to roast the turkey, place it on a rack set in a rimmed baking sheet. In a small bowl, blend the salt, pepper, herbes de Provence, lemon zest, and sage and rub all over the turkey, including in the cavity. Refrigerate, uncovered, for 2 days. 2. Remove the turkey from the refrigerator at least 1 hour before you plan to roast it. Stuff the cavity with the onion, celery, and garlic. Tuck the wings under the breast and tie the legs together with kitchen twine. Brush the turkey with the melted butter. 3. To install the grill grate, position it flat on top of the heating element so it sits in place. 4. Select the ROAST function. Adjust the temperature to 325°F and time to 3 hours. Select START/STOP to begin preheating. 5. When preheating is complete, open the hood and place the turkey on the grill grate. Once the hood is closed, cooking will begin and the timer will begin counting down. 6. Roast the turkey until the juices run clear and the internal temperature at the thigh reaches 165°F. 7. Transfer the turkey to a cutting board and loosely tent with aluminum foil. Let rest for 1 hour, then carve and serve.

Aromatic Tea-Smoked Whole Duck

Prep Time: 10 minutes | Cook Time: 2 hours | Serves: 6

½ cup loose tea leaves
5 whole cloves
3 whole star anise
2 tablespoons grated orange zest
¼ cup thawed frozen orange juice concentrate

1 tablespoon tamari
1 tablespoon rice wine vinegar
½ teaspoon kosher salt
¼ teaspoon ground cinnamon
1 (5- to 6-pound) duck

1. Using a spice grinder, coffee grinder, or mortar and pestle, grind the tea leaves, cloves, and star anise together into a fine powder, then stir in the orange zest. Pour the tea blend into a small bowl and whisk in the juice concentrate, tamari, vinegar, salt, and cinnamon. Let the mixture stand at room temperature for 30 minutes or cover and refrigerate for up to 2 hours. 2. Cut any excess fat from the duck cavity and pin any excess skin under the duck by folding the wing tips under. Smear the tea paste over the duck, including some in the cavity. Let stand at room temperature for 1 hour or cover with plastic wrap and refrigerate for up to 4 hours. 3. To install the grill grate, position it flat on top of the heating element so it sits in place. 4. Place the duck on the grill grate, then close the hood. 5. Use the pellet scoop to pour pellets into the smoke box until filled to the top. Select SMOKER. Set grill temperature to 500°F and time to 2 hours. Select START/STOP to begin cooking. Cook until the duck is a beautiful mahogany and the internal temperature at the thigh registers 150° to 160° F, about 2 hours. 6. Transfer the duck to a cutting board and let rest for about 30 minutes. Cut into serving portions and serve hot or at room temperature.

Smoky Whole Chicken

Prep Time: 10 minutes | Cook Time: 3 hours | Serves: 8

2 (3½- to 4-pound) whole chickens
2 tablespoons vegetable oil
⅓ cup paprika
¼ cup chili powder
1 tablespoon salt
1 tablespoon onion powder

2 teaspoons ground cumin
2 teaspoons dry mustard
2 teaspoons granulated garlic
2 teaspoons freshly ground black pepper
2 teaspoons dried parsley
1 teaspoon dried thyme

1. Trim away any excess skin, blot chickens dry with paper towels, and brush them all over with vegetable oil. 2. Combine the paprika, chili powder, salt, onion powder, cumin, dry mustard, granulated garlic, black pepper, parsley, and thyme in a small bowl. Divide the mixture in half, and use one half to season each chicken. Massage the rub under the breast skin and inside the cavity as well. 3. To install the grill grate, position it flat on top of the heating element so it sits in place. Plug thermometer into the top jack labeled "1" on the left side of the control panel. 4. Place chickens on the grill grate, then close the hood. 5. Use the pellet scoop to pour pellets into the smoke box until filled to the top. Select SMOKER. Set grill temperature to 250°F and time to 3 hours. Set the thermometer to CHICKEN. Select START/STOP to begin cooking. Once the chickens reach 195°F in the thigh area and 185°F in the breast area, they are done. 6. Remove the chickens from the smoker and let them rest for 10 minutes before carving and serving. Use heat-resistant food-safe gloves if you are planning on pulling the chicken.

Smoked Sweet Turkey Legs

Prep Time: 30 minutes | Cook Time: 3 hours | Serves: 4

8 cups water
½ cup bourbon
½ cup kosher salt
½ cup white sugar
2 bay leaves
4 cups ice, plus more if needed

4 turkey legs
¼ cup sriracha or other chili sauce
⅔ cup brown sugar
½ cup Beef and Game Rub, salt omitted
½ cup apple juice
¼ cup apple cider vinegar

1. In a large stockpot over medium-high heat, add the water, bourbon, salt, and white sugar. Simmer for 3 to 4 minutes. Remove from heat and add the bay leaves and ice. Let the mixture cool completely. Add another cup of ice if needed. Once cooled, submerge the turkey legs in the brine, cover, and place into the refrigerator for 12 to 18 hours. 2. Remove the legs from the brine and lightly rinse them under cold water. Blot dry with paper towels. Brush about 1 tablespoon of sriracha onto each leg. 3. In a medium bowl, combine the brown sugar with the saltless Beef and Game Rub. Apply the rub all over the turkey legs. 4. To install the grill grate, position it flat on top of the heating element so it sits in place. 5. Place the turkey legs on the grill grate, then close the hood. 6. Use the pellet scoop to pour pellets into the smoke box until filled to the top. Select SMOKER. Set grill temperature to 250°F and time to 3 hours. Select START/STOP to begin cooking. 7. Pour the apple juice and apple cider vinegar into a spray bottle. After 1½ to 2 hours of cook time, spritz the legs with this mixture every 30 minutes. 8. Once cooked, place the legs on a large platter or cutting board. Tent with foil, and let them rest for 10 minutes before digging in.

Smoked Turkey & Poblano Poppers

Prep Time: 30 minutes | Cook Time: 4 hours | Serves: 8

For the Savory Rice:
1 tablespoon unsalted butter
1 tablespoon extra-virgin olive oil
1 cup diced yellow onion
Flaked sea salt
Freshly ground black pepper
For the Poppers:
2 andouille sausages, casings removed and thinly sliced
2 Roma tomatoes, quartered lengthwise, seeded, and diced
2 scallions, trimmed and thinly sliced on an angle
2 cups shredded Monterey Jack cheese
8 poblano peppers, halved lengthwise, ribbed, and seeded
2 (4-pound) fresh bone-in skin-on turkey breasts

2 cups long-grain white or brown rice
1 tablespoon fresh thyme leaves, stripped and finely chopped
1 fresh bay leaf
4 cups chicken (or vegetable) stock

Flaked sea salt
Freshly ground black pepper
4 limes, halved
Finely chopped fresh cilantro leaves, for garnish
Sour cream, for garnish

To make the savory rice: 1. Preheat a large saucepan over medium-high heat. 2. In the pan, combine the butter, olive oil, and onion. Season with salt and pepper. Sauté the onion for about 10 minutes, until golden brown. 3. Add the rice, thyme, and bay leaf, stirring to coat the rice in the butter and oil. 4. Add the chicken stock. Stir gently, cover the pan, and reduce the heat to low. Cook for 45 to 60 minutes, until the liquid is absorbed. Remove and discard the bay leaf.
To make the poppers: 1. In a large bowl, fold together the sausage, tomatoes, scallions, 4 cups of the savory rice, and Monterey Jack cheese. Spoon the mixture into the pepper halves, mounding and gently pressing to fill the cavity. 2. To install the grill grate, position it flat on top of the heating element so it sits in place. 3. Arrange the stuffed peppers in a single layer, spaced evenly without touching, on the grill grate; Season the turkey all over with salt and pepper. Place the turkey breasts on the grill grate, spaced evenly without touching. Then close the hood. 4. Use the pellet scoop to pour pellets into the smoke box until filled to the top. Select SMOKER. Set grill temperature to 275°F and time to 4 hours. Select START/STOP to begin cooking. 5. Let the turkey cool slightly. Gently remove the bones and thinly slice across the breast on an angle. 6. Top the stuffed peppers with turkey slices. Serve with lime halves, fresh cilantro, and sour cream.

All-American Smoked Turkey

Prep Time: 15 minutes | Cook Time: 2 hour 30 minutes | Serves: 10

1 (13- to 16-pound) whole turkey
2 tablespoons olive oil

Poultry Rub

1. Rub the turkey with the olive oil and generously season with the rub. Rub the seasoning under the skin, if you can. 2. To install the grill grate, position it flat on top of the heating element so it sits in place. 3. Place the turkey on the grill grate, then close the hood. 4. Use the pellet scoop to pour pellets into the smoke box until filled to the top. Select SMOKER. Set grill temperature to 375°F and time to 2½ hours. Select START/STOP to begin cooking. Cook until the internal temperature reaches 170°F. 5. Remove the turkey from the grill and let rest for 10 minutes. 6. Carve and serve.

Delicious Caramelized Orange Duck

Prep Time: 25 minutes | Cook Time: 2 hours | Serves: 4

1 (4- to 5-pound) duck
⅓ cup kosher salt
½ cup orange marmalade
2 tablespoons freshly squeezed lemon juice

¼ cup maple syrup
2 tablespoons water
1 teaspoon soy sauce
Pinch ground cloves

1. Remove the giblets from inside the duck. Blot the duck dry with paper towels and set on a baking sheet. Using a metal skewer or sturdy toothpick, puncture the skin (but not the flesh) several times all over the duck, and rub it with salt. Place the sheet with the duck into the refrigerator, uncovered, for 12 to 15 hours. 2. Once brined, remove the duck from the refrigerator and wipe away the salt with paper towels. Blot the surface dry. 3. To install the grill grate, position it flat on top of the heating element so it sits in place. 4. Place duck on the grill grate, then close the hood. 5. Use the pellet scoop to pour pellets into the smoke box until filled to the top. Select SMOKER. Set grill temperature to 275°F and time to 2 hours. Select START/STOP to begin cooking. 6. Meanwhile, in a small saucepan over medium heat, bring the orange marmalade, lemon juice, maple syrup, water, soy sauce, and cloves to a simmer. Stir until all the marmalade and maple syrup have melted and incorporated and the mixture is heated through. Cover and keep warm. 7. Preheat the oven to broil when the duck is almost done cooking. Baste the duck with the orange sauce and place it under the broiler for a few minutes until it caramelizes. Let the duck rest for 10 minutes, carve, and plate. If you have leftover orange sauce, serve it on the side.

Tasty Chicken Cacciatore

Prep Time: 20 minutes | Cook Time: 4 hours | Serves: 4

2 chickens, whole, separated into breasts, thighs, legs, and wings
All-purpose flour, for dusting
Flaked sea salt
Freshly ground black pepper
2 tablespoons extra-virgin olive oil
1 yellow onion, thinly sliced
1 green bell pepper, trimmed, seeded, and thinly sliced
1 red bell pepper, trimmed, seeded, and thinly sliced
12 white mushrooms, or cremini mushrooms, brushed clean,

stemmed, and quartered
8 garlic cloves, very thinly sliced
2 tablespoons tomato paste
1 cup white wine
4 Roma tomatoes, quartered and diced
2 rosemary sprigs, leaves stripped and finely chopped
2 oregano sprigs, leaves stripped and finely chopped
1 cup chicken (or vegetable) stock

1. Pat the chicken dry with a paper towel. Lightly dust the chicken with flour and season it with salt and pepper. 2. To install the grill grate, position it flat on top of the heating element so it sits in place. Plug thermometer into the top jack labeled "1" on the left side of the control panel. 3. Place the chicken on the grill grate, leaving space between each piece, then close the hood. 4. Use the pellet scoop to pour pellets into the smoke box until filled to the top. Select SMOKER. Set grill temperature to 275°F and time to 2 hours. Set the thermometer to CHICKEN. Select START/STOP to begin cooking. Cook until the internal temperature reaches 165°F. Then remove to a plate. 5. In a large baking pan, gently stir together the olive oil, onion, green and red bell peppers, mushrooms, and garlic. Season with salt and pepper. Stir in the tomato paste. Place the pan on the grill grate. Smoke the vegetables at 275°F for about 1 hour, until tender. 6. Stir in the white wine to deglaze the pan, scraping up any browned bits from the bottom. 7. Add the tomatoes, rosemary, oregano, and chicken stock to the pan. Stir to combine. 8. Nestle the smoked chicken into the pan and return it to the smoker. Smoke at the same setting for 1 hour, or until tender and the sauce is reduced to a velvety consistency.

Smoked Duck Breasts

Prep Time: 15 minutes | Cook Time: 2½ hours | Serves: 8

4 boneless, skin-on duck breasts
1-quart apple juice
2 tablespoons coarse kosher salt
2 tablespoons brown sugar
2 tablespoons soy sauce
1 teaspoon onion powder

1 teaspoon paprika
1 teaspoon granulated garlic
1 teaspoon dried marjoram
½ teaspoon five-spice powder
½ teaspoon white pepper

1. Place the duck breasts into a large plastic bowl or glass baking dish. 2. In a large bowl, combine the apple juice, salt, sugar, soy sauce, onion powder, paprika, granulated garlic, marjoram, five-spice powder, and white pepper, and stir until the salt and sugar have dissolved. Pour the marinade over the duck breasts, seal with plastic wrap, and refrigerate for 4 to 5 hours. 3. To install the grill grate, position it flat on top of the heating element so it sits in place. 4. Remove the duck breasts from the refrigerator and discard the excess marinade. Lightly pat the duck breasts dry, then place them on the grill grate skin-side up, then close the hood. 5. Use the pellet scoop to pour pellets into the smoke box until filled to the top. Select SMOKER. Set grill temperature to250°F and time to 2½ hours. Select START/STOP to begin cooking. 6. Remove from the smoker, place onto a cutting board, and tent loosely with aluminum foil. Rest them for 10 minutes, slice, and serve.

Easy Smoked Duck Legs

Prep Time: 20 minutes | Cook Time: 3 hours | Serves: 4

4 duck leg quarters, Muscovy or Pekin
2 tablespoons kosher salt, divided, plus more as needed

2 teaspoons freshly ground black pepper

1. Pat the duck legs dry with paper towels. Using a sharp skewer, prick the skin in several spots, making sure not to puncture the flesh. Rub each leg with ½ tablespoon kosher salt, then place them into a glass baking dish or large plastic container. Cover with plastic wrap, and refrigerate for 12 hours. 2. Remove the duck legs from the refrigerator and wipe away the salt and moisture with paper towels. Season with black pepper. 3. To install the grill grate, position it flat on top of the heating element so it sits in place. 4. Place the duck legs on the grill grate, skin-side up, then close the hood. 5. Use the pellet scoop to pour pellets into the smoke box until filled to the top. Select SMOKER. Set grill temperature to 250°F and time to 3 hours. Select START/STOP to begin cooking. Cook until they reach an internal temperature of 180°F. 6. Once cooked, place the legs onto a plate or serving dish and let them rest for 15 minutes. Serve as is, or shred and use in other dishes.

Chicken and Sausage Jambalaya

Prep Time: 35 minutes | Cook Time: 45 minutes | Serves: 8

For the Spice Blend:
1 tablespoon smoked paprika
2 teaspoons fresh thyme
1½ teaspoons cayenne pepper

1 teaspoon dried oregano
1 teaspoon kosher salt

For the Jambalaya:
1 skin-on, bone-in chicken breast
1 chicken leg (with thigh attached)
Kosher salt
4 bacon slices
12 ounces smoked sausage, such as andouille, cut into ¼-inch-thick rounds
1 bunch scallions, white and green parts, finely chopped
2 celery stalks, finely diced

1 green bell pepper, seeded and finely diced
6 garlic cloves, chopped
1½ cups long-grain white rice
4 cups low-sodium chicken broth
2 bay leaves
Few dashes your favorite hot sauce
Freshly ground black pepper
¼ cup chopped fresh flat-leaf parsley, for garnish

To make the spice blend: In a small bowl, mix together the paprika, thyme, cayenne, oregano, and salt.
To make the gumbo: 1. Season the chicken breast and leg generously with salt. Refrigerate overnight. 2. Pat the chicken dry. Put the bacon and sausage in a baking pan. 3. To install grill grate, position it flat on top of the heating element so it sits in place, then close hood. Use pellet scoop to pour pellets into smoke box until filled to top. 4. Select GRILL. Select WOODFIRE FLAVOR. Set grill temperature to HI. Set the time to 2 minutes. Select START/STOP to begin preheating. 5. When unit beeps to signify it has preheated and ADD FOOD displays, open hood and place the pan on the grill grate. Close hood and grill for 2 minutes or until the bacon is browned and crispy around the edges. Transfer to a plate. Once cool enough to handle, crumble the bacon. 6. Add the chicken skin-side down in a single layer in the pan. Close the grill hood and cook for 8 to 10 minutes or until the skin is browned. Transfer to a plate. 7. Add the scallions, celery, bell pepper, and garlic and stir to combine. Close the grill hood and cook, stirring occasionally, for 6 to 7 minutes or until slightly softened. Remove from the grill. 8. Wearing barbecue gloves, carefully remove the grate, install the heat deflector, and replace the grate. Reduce the grill temperature to 400°F. 9. Put the pan back on the grate. Add the rice, broth, chicken, bacon, sausage, bay leaves, spice blend, and hot sauce. Season with pepper. Close the hood and cook for 30 to 35 minutes or until the rice is tender, the liquid is fully absorbed. 10. Garnish with the parsley and serve immediately.

Apricot Jam-Glazed Cornish Game Hens

Prep Time: 15 minutes | Cook Time: 1½ to 2 hours | Serves: 4

4 Cornish game hens
2 tablespoons olive oil, divided
1 tablespoon salt, divided
1 tablespoon freshly ground black pepper, divided
1 cup apricot jam

1 tablespoon dry mustard
1 tablespoon sherry vinegar
2 tablespoons olive oil
¼ teaspoon cayenne pepper

1. Trim any loose pieces of skin from the hens. Brush each one with ½ tablespoon olive oil and season with salt and pepper. Set aside. 2. To install the grill grate, position it flat on top of the heating element so it sits in place. 3. Place the hens on the grill grate, then close the hood. 4. Use the pellet scoop to pour pellets into the smoke box until filled to the top. Select SMOKER. Set grill temperature to 225°F and time to 2 hours. Select START/STOP to begin cooking. 5. Meanwhile, prepare the glaze by combining the apricot jam, dry mustard, sherry vinegar, olive oil, and cayenne in a small saucepan over low heat. Warm through for about 10 minutes or until well combined. 6. Once the hens reach a temperature of 165°F (about 1½ to 2 hours), brush them liberally with the apricot glaze and continue cooking until the glaze forms a thick, sticky surface, about 10 minutes. 7. Remove, rest for 5 to 10 minutes, and serve.

Roasted Orange Goose

Prep Time: 10 minutes | Cook Time: 2½ hours | Serves: 6

1 (9- to 11-pound) goose
1 orange, cut in half
1 teaspoon ground allspice

Kosher salt and freshly ground black pepper
½ cup maple syrup (grade B preferred)
¼ cup orange-flavored liqueur

1. Remove the giblets and any obvious fat from the goose. With an ice pick or metal skewer, puncture the skin of the goose all over. This will let excess fat render out of the goose. Rub the orange halves all over the goose, inside and out, squeezing the juice out as you do. Place the orange halves inside the cavity. Season the goose inside and out with the allspice and salt and pepper to taste. Cover with plastic wrap and refrigerate for 24 hours. 2. Remove the bird from the refrigerator at least 1 hour before you plan to roast. Cross the legs and tie them together with kitchen twine and put the wing joints under the bird. Place the bird on a baking pan. 3. To install the grill grate, position it flat on top of the heating element so it sits in place. 4. Select the ROAST function. Adjust the temperature to 500°F and time to 30 minutes. Select START/STOP to begin preheating. 5. When preheating is complete, open the hood and place the baking pan on the grill grate. Once the hood is closed, cooking will begin and the timer will begin counting down. 6. Roast for about 30 minutes. Then adjust the temperature to 350°F and roast for 1 hour, then baste with the maple syrup. Roast for about another hour, basting every 30 minutes, alternating between the maple syrup and pan juices each time. The bird is done when the juices run clear and the internal temperature at the thigh is 165° F; figure on 20 minutes per pound. 7. Transfer the goose to a cutting board and let rest for 15 minutes before carving.

Soy-Marinated Chicken

Prep Time: 15 minutes | Cook Time: 20 minutes | Serves: 4

8 boneless, skinless chicken thighs
¼ cup soy sauce
3 tablespoons toasted sesame oil
2 tablespoons minced garlic

1 tablespoon peeled grated fresh ginger
1 tablespoon rice vinegar
2 teaspoons coarse ground black pepper

1. Slice the chicken into thin, even pieces, about ½ inch thick, and remove any unwanted fat. 2. In a large bowl, whisk together the soy sauce, oil, garlic, ginger, vinegar, and pepper. Add the chicken pieces and combine until the marinade is evenly incorporated. Cover and refrigerate the bowl and let the chicken marinate for at least 4 hours, although 24 hours is best. 3. To install grill grate, position it flat on top of the heating element so it sits in place, then close hood. Use pellet scoop to pour pellets into smoke box until filled to top. 4. Select GRILL. Select WOODFIRE FLAVOR. Set grill temperature to HI. Set the time to 20 minutes. Select START/STOP to begin preheating. 5. When unit beeps to signify it has preheated and ADD FOOD displays, shake off and discard any excess marinade from the chicken. 6. Open hood and place the chicken on the grill grate. Close hood and grill for 20 minutes, flipping halfway through. Grill until the juice runs clear and there is no pink in the center.

Herbed Goat Cheese-Stuffed Chicken Breasts

Prep Time: 10 minutes | Cook Time: 20 minutes | Serves: 4

4 ounces fresh soft goat cheese
1 tablespoon finely chopped fresh tarragon
1 tablespoon finely chopped fresh parsley
1 tablespoon finely chopped fresh chives
1 teaspoon finely chopped fresh oregano
1 tablespoon extra-virgin olive oil, plus more for brushing

Kosher salt and freshly ground black pepper
4 bone-in chicken breast halves
Kitchen twine or toothpicks
½ cup pear preserves or more as needed
Dash of vanilla extract

1. In a small bowl, mash the goat cheese, herbs, olive oil, and a sprinkling of salt and pepper together with a fork until thoroughly combined. 2. One at a time, take the chicken breasts and sit each one on its rib bones. Make an incision horizontally almost through the breast. Season the breasts with salt and black pepper, then divide the goat cheese mixture among the breasts. Fold the breasts back together and tie a couple of loops around each breast or insert a toothpick or two to hold each breast together. Cover with plastic wrap and refrigerate for 24 hours. 3. In a small saucepan, heat the pear preserves over low heat until loose. Add the vanilla and taste, adding more if you like. Set aside. (Any leftovers are great on toasted bread.) 4. To install grill grate, position it flat on top of the heating element so it sits in place, then close hood. Use pellet scoop to pour pellets into smoke box until filled to top. 5. Select GRILL. Select WOODFIRE FLAVOR. Set grill temperature to HI. Set the time to 20 minutes. Select START/STOP to begin preheating. 6. When unit beeps to signify it has preheated and ADD FOOD displays, remove the breasts from the refrigerator and brush both sides with olive oil. Place on the grill grate, skin side down. Close hood and grill for 20 minutes, flipping halfway through. When the chicken is pressed, it should feel somewhat firm, and an instant-read thermometer inserted in the center should read 165° F. 7. Transfer the breasts to a platter, pull out the twine or toothpicks, and serve with at least a tablespoon of pear preserves over the top of each breast.

Smoked BBQ Chicken

Prep Time: 30 minutes | Cook Time: 3 hours | Serves: 6

1 fryer chicken, cut in half or into pieces
Kosher salt

Freshly ground black pepper
1½ cups Ballistic BBQ Sauce

1. Season all sides of the chicken with a few pinches of salt and pepper. 2. To install the grill grate, position it flat on top of the heating element so it sits in place. Plug thermometer into the top jack labeled "1" on the left side of the control panel. 3. Place the chicken on the grill grate, then close the hood. 4. Use the pellet scoop to pour pellets into the smoke box until filled to the top. Select SMOKER. Set grill temperature to 250°F and time to 3 hours. Set the thermometer to CHICKEN. Select START/STOP to begin cooking. 5. Cook until the chicken reaches 150°F at the thigh, and adjust the temperature to 300°F. 6. When the internal temperature of the chicken reaches 170°F, remove the chicken from the smoker and baste it with the glaze. Then put it back in the smoker, with the vent over the meat. 7. Once the internal temperature of the chicken reaches 175°F, remove it from the smoker and serve.

Lime-Honey Smoked Chicken Wings

Prep Time: 30 minutes | Cook Time: 2 hours | Serves: 6

3 limes, thinly sliced, plus 3 limes, quartered lengthwise, for serving
¼ cup coarse sea salt
¼ cup wildflower honey
1 jalapeño pepper, thinly sliced, plus more for additional heat (optional)
2 tablespoons fresh thyme leaves, stripped and finely chopped

3 fresh bay leaves
3 (12-ounce) bottles pilsner beer
6 pounds bone-in skin-on chicken wings, rinsed and drained
Flaked sea salt
Freshly ground black pepper

1. In a large bowl, stir together the lime slices, coarse sea salt, honey, jalapeño, thyme, lime, bay leaves, and beer. Transfer to a large food-grade plastic bag and add the wings. Remove as much air as possible from the bag and seal it. Refrigerate for 24 hours, turning the bag occasionally. 2. Drain the wings and pat them dry. 3. To install the grill grate, position it flat on top of the heating element so it sits in place. 4. Arrange the wings on the grill grate, leaving space between each one, top with additional jalapeño, if desired. Season with salt and pepper. Then close the hood. 5. Use the pellet scoop to pour pellets into the smoke box until filled to the top. Select SMOKER. Set grill temperature to 275°F and time to 2 hours. Select START/STOP to begin cooking. 6. Serve with lime wedges on the side.

Lemon-Honey Smoked Chicken

Prep Time: 20 minutes | Cook Time: 2 hours 15 minutes| Serves: 4

4 boneless skinless chicken breasts
2 tablespoons extra-virgin olive oil
Flaked sea salt
Freshly ground black pepper
Grated zest of 2 lemons, plus juice of 2 lemons, plus 2 lemons,

halved, for serving
4 thyme sprigs, leaves stripped and finely chopped, plus more for garnish
¼ cup clover honey

1. Pat the chicken dry with a paper towel. Brush the chicken all over with the olive oil. Season all sides of the chicken with salt, pepper, lemon zest, and thyme. 2. To install the grill grate, position it flat on top of the heating element so it sits in place. 3. Arrange the chicken, breast-side up, on the grill grate, leaving space between each piece. Then close the hood. 4. Use the pellet scoop to pour pellets into the smoke box until filled to the top. Select SMOKER. Set grill temperature to 275°F and time to 2 hours. Select START/STOP to begin cooking. 5. Squeeze the juice of the zested lemons over the chicken and drizzle with the honey. Smoke for 15 minutes more. Garnish with fresh thyme. Serve with additional lemon halves for squeezing.

Smoked Chicken and Celery Salad

Prep Time: 10 minutes | Cook Time: 45 minutes | Serves: 8

2 pounds boneless, skinless chicken breasts
1 tablespoon olive oil
Kosher salt
Freshly ground black pepper

1 cup mayonnaise
3 celery stalks, minced
3 scallions, sliced

1. Coat the chicken with olive oil and season both sides with salt and pepper. 2. To install the grill grate, position it flat on top of the heating element so it sits in place. 3. Place the chicken on the grill grate, then close the hood. 4. Use the pellet scoop to pour pellets into the smoke box until filled to the top. Select SMOKER. Set grill temperature to 250°F and time to 45 minutes. Select START/STOP to begin cooking. 5. Remove the chicken from the grill, let cool, then dice it and place in a large bowl. Add the mayonnaise, celery, and scallions. Taste for seasoning and add more salt and pepper if needed.

Grilled Citrus Chicken

Prep Time: 10 minutes | Cook Time: 24 minutes | Serves: 4

For the Marinade:

1 cup pineapple juice
¼ cup orange juice
2 tablespoons freshly squeezed lime juice
2 tablespoons light brown sugar
1 tablespoon kosher salt
1 tablespoon white vinegar

2 teaspoons chili powder
1 teaspoon dried oregano
½ teaspoon freshly ground black pepper
½ teaspoon cayenne pepper
1 teaspoon granulated garlic
2 tablespoons canola oil

1. Place the chicken thighs in a gallon-size zip-top bag and pour in the pineapple, orange, and lime juices. Add the brown sugar, salt, vinegar, chili powder, oregano, black pepper, cayenne, and garlic. Seal the bag while pressing out any air. Massage the marinade over the chicken and refrigerate it for at least 2 hours. 2. To install grill grate, position it flat on top of the heating element so it sits in place, then close hood. Use pellet scoop to pour pellets into smoke box until filled to top. 3. Select GRILL. Select WOODFIRE FLAVOR. Set grill temperature to HI. Set the time to 14 minutes. Select START/STOP to begin preheating. 4. When unit beeps to signify it has preheated and ADD FOOD displays, on the open hood and remove the chicken from the marinade and place it, skin-side down on the grill grate. Close hood and grill for 24 minutes, flipping halfway through. 5. Remove the chicken from the grill, cover loosely with aluminum foil, and let the chicken rest for 5 minutes before serving.

Grilled Spiced Chicken

Prep Time: 20 minutes | Cook Time: 20 minutes | Serves: 4

8 boneless, skinless chicken thighs
2 tablespoons gochujang
2 tablespoons coarse gochugaru flakes
2 tablespoons minced garlic
2 teaspoons peeled grated fresh ginger

2 tablespoons toasted sesame oil
2 tablespoons lightly packed dark brown sugar
2 tablespoons soy sauce
1 teaspoon kosher salt

1. Slice the chicken into thin, even pieces, about ½ inch thick, and remove any unwanted fat. 2. In a large bowl, whisk together the gochujang, gochugaru, garlic, ginger, oil, brown sugar, soy sauce, and salt. Add the chicken pieces and combine until the marinade is evenly incorporated. Cover and refrigerate the bowl and let the chicken marinate for at least 4 hours, although 24 hours is best. 3. To install grill grate, position it flat on top of the heating element so it sits in place, then close hood. Use pellet scoop to pour pellets into smoke box until filled to top. 4. Select GRILL. Select WOODFIRE FLAVOR. Set grill temperature to HI. Set the time to 20 minutes. Select START/STOP to begin preheating. 5. When unit beeps to signify it has preheated and ADD FOOD displays, open hood and shake off and discard any excess marinade from the chicken. Place the chicken on the grill grate. Close hood and grill for 20 minutes, flipping halfway through. Make sure not to move them around too much so that you can get some browning, until the juice runs clear and there is no pink in the center.

Delicious Thanksgiving Turkey

Prep Time: 10 minutes | Cook Time: 3½ hours | Serves: 12

1 (12- to 14-pound) fresh turkey
½ cup dried herbes de Provence
¼ cup kosher salt
2 tablespoons freshly ground black pepper

1 large carrot, cut into thirds
1 rib celery, cut into thirds
1 medium onion, cut into quarters
1 lemon

1. Remove the giblets and neck from the turkey and reserve for another use, such as making a giblet gravy, if desired. Rinse the turkey thoroughly with cold water and pat dry. In a small bowl, combine the herbes de Provence, salt, and pepper. Heavily coat the outside of the bird and the cavity with this mixture. Place on a rack, set the rack in a disposable aluminum-foil pan, cover with plastic wrap, and refrigerate 24 to 48 hours. 2. Remove the turkey from the refrigerator at least 1 hour before you plan to cook. Stuff the cavity with the carrot, celery, and onion pieces. Cut the lemon in half, squeeze the juices over the breast of the bird, and stuff the rinds into the cavity. Fold the wings under the bird and tie the legs together with kitchen twine. 3. To install the grill grate, position it flat on top of the heating element so it sits in place. 4. Place the turkey in a baking pan and place the pan on the grill grate, then close the hood. 5. Use the pellet scoop to pour pellets into the smoke box until filled to the top. Select SMOKER. Set grill temperature to 225°F and time to 3½ hours. Select START/STOP to begin cooking. 6. The juices should run clear when the thigh is pierced with a skewer. Remove from the grill, tent with aluminum foil, and let rest for about 1 hour before carving. If desired, use the accumulated pan juices to make your gravy. When ready to carve, remove the lemon, onion, celery, and carrot from the cavity. Carve however desired.

Smoked Herb-Garlic Chicken

Prep Time: 20 minutes | Cook Time: 3 hours | Serves: 4

2 chickens, whole
¼ cup ground ancho chile pepper
2 tablespoons paprika
2 tablespoons ground coriander
4 thyme sprigs, leaves stripped and finely chopped

4 rosemary sprigs, leaves stripped and finely chopped
8 garlic cloves, finely chopped
Extra-virgin olive oil, for drizzling
Flaked sea salt
Freshly ground black pepper

1. To prepare the chickens, place them breast-side down on a cutting board. Working one at a time, locate the spine. Using poultry shears or heavy-duty kitchen shears, cut on either side of the spine, one side at a time, cutting as close to the spine as possible. Remove the spine and separate the chicken halves. Repeat. 2. In a large bowl, whisk together the chile pepper, paprika, coriander, thyme, rosemary, and garlic. Set aside. 3. Rinse the chicken in cold water and pat it dry with a paper towel. Drizzle the chicken all over with olive oil and season with salt and pepper. 4. Completely coat the chicken with the spice mixture, rubbing the mixture into the skin and flesh. 5. To install the grill grate, position it flat on top of the heating element so it sits in place. Plug thermometer into the top jack labeled "1" on the left side of the control panel. 6. Place the chicken, skin-side down, on the grill grate. Place 1 brick on top of each chicken half, then close the hood. 7. Use the pellet scoop to pour pellets into the smoke box until filled to the top. Select SMOKER. Set grill temperature to 275°F and time to 3 hours. Set the thermometer to CHICKEN. Select START/STOP to begin cooking. Cook until the internal temperature reaches 165°F. 8. Gently remove the chicken from the grill grate, being careful to keep the skin intact.

Prunes-Smoked Chicken

Prep Time: 30 minutes | Cook Time: 3 hours | Serves: 8

½ cup red wine vinegar
¼ cup extra-virgin olive oil
1 cup dried pitted prunes
½ cup capers
½ cup pitted green olives
6 garlic cloves, minced
¼ cup fresh oregano leaves, finely chopped
3 fresh or dried bay leaves

2 (3- to 4-pound) chickens, whole, separated into breasts, legs, thighs, and wings
Flaked sea salt
Freshly ground black pepper
2 cups sauvignon blanc or Riesling
½ cup packed light brown sugar
¼ cup fresh flat-leaf parsley leaves, finely chopped

1. In a large bowl, whisk together the vinegar, olive oil, prunes, capers, olives, garlic, oregano, and bay leaves. Add the chicken and turn to coat. Cover the bowl with plastic wrap and refrigerate for 24 hours, turning the chicken 2 or 3 times. 2. Strain the chicken and pat it dry, reserving the marinade in the refrigerator. Season the chicken on both sides with salt and pepper. 3. To install the grill grate, position it flat on top of the heating element so it sits in place. Plug thermometer into the top jack labeled "1" on the left side of the control panel. 4. Arrange the chicken on the grill grate, skin-side up, leaving space between each piece. Then close the hood. 5. Use the pellet scoop to pour pellets into the smoke box until filled to the top. Select SMOKER. Set grill temperature to 275°F and time to 2 hours. Set the thermometer to CHICKEN. Select START/STOP to begin cooking. Smoke until the internal temperature reaches 165°F. 6. Once done smoking, arrange the chicken in a single layer in a baking pan and coat it evenly with the reserved marinade. 7. Pour in the white wine and sprinkle the chicken evenly with the sugar. Return the chicken to the smoker for 60 to 90 minutes, basting it occasionally, until the sauce reaches the desired consistency. 8. Serve topped with fresh parsley and the prune and olive pan sauce. Remove and discard the bay leaves.

Citrus Duck with Plums

Prep Time: 20 minutes | Cook Time: 3 hours | Serves: 4

2 tablespoons canola oil
1 duck, whole
Flaked sea salt
Freshly ground black pepper
4 mandarin oranges, halved, divided
8 thyme sprigs, divided

8 blue plums, halved and pitted
8 shallots, halved
4 star anise, whole
4 cloves, whole
2 cinnamon sticks, whole
1 (750-mL) bottle sauvignon blanc

1. Coat a baking pan with canola oil. Season the duck all over, inside and out, with salt and pepper. Stuff the cavity with 4 orange halves and 4 thyme sprigs. Set the duck in the prepared pan, breast-side up. 2. Arrange the plums, shallots, star anise, cloves, cinnamon sticks, remaining 4 orange halves, and remaining 4 thyme sprigs around the duck. 3. Pour the white wine over the ingredients surrounding the duck. Season with salt and pepper. 4. To install the grill grate, position it flat on top of the heating element so it sits in place. 5. Place the pan on the grill grate, then close the hood. 6. Use the pellet scoop to pour pellets into the smoke box until filled to the top. Select SMOKER. Set grill temperature to 275°F and time to 2 hours. Select START/STOP to begin cooking. Open the smoker occasionally to spoon the rendered liquids over the entire dish. Continue to smoke for 1 to 2 hours more, or until the internal temperature reaches 165°F. 7. Remove the duck from the smoker, loosely tent it with aluminum foil, and let it rest for 20 minutes. 8. Remove and discard the thyme, star anise, and cinnamon sticks. Serve the duck with a side of the plums and shallots.

Smoked Jerk Chicken

Prep Time: 15 minutes | Cook Time: 3 hours | Serves: 4

1 (4- to 5-pound) whole chicken

¾ cup jerk marinade

1. Pat the chicken dry. Place it breast-side up on a cutting board with the legs facing you, so the cavity is visible. Using poultry shears, cut along the bottom of the cavity on each side of the backbone and neck to release them; remove and discard. Using the palms of your hands, flatten the breasts. Transfer to a shallow dish. 2. Pour the marinade over the chicken and rub it evenly into the flesh on both sides. Refrigerate overnight. 3. To install the grill grate, position it flat on top of the heating element so it sits in place. 4. Place the chicken skin-side up on the grill grate, then close the hood. 5. Use the pellet scoop to pour pellets into the smoke box until filled to the top. Select SMOKER. Set grill temperature to 250°F and time to 2½ hours. Select START/STOP to begin cooking. 6. Rest for 10 minutes before serving. Carve off the breasts, thighs, legs, and wings; cut the breasts into slices and serve.

Garlic Sage-Rubbed Turkey Breast

Prep Time: 15 minutes | Cook Time: 1 hour | Serves: 6

1 tablespoon poultry seasoning
1 tablespoon dried sage
1 tablespoon garlic powder
1 teaspoon salt

½ teaspoon black pepper
1 (3-pound) frozen boneless turkey breast, thawed
4 tablespoons (½ stick) butter, melted

1. In a small bowl, stir together the poultry seasoning, sage, garlic powder, salt, and pepper until combined. Pat the turkey breast dry with a paper towel. Coat the entire turkey breast with melted butter. Evenly distribute the seasoning mix over the entire surface of the turkey breast. Cover and let sit at room temperature for 30 minutes. 2. To install the grill grate, position it flat on top of the heating element so it sits in place. 3. Oil the grill grate and place the turkey on the grill grate, then close the hood. 4. Use the pellet scoop to pour pellets into the smoke box until filled to the top. Select SMOKER. Set grill temperature to 375°F and time to 1 hour. Select START/STOP to begin cooking, turning every 30 minutes, until the internal temperature reaches 150°F. Move the turkey breast to the hot side and cook for 2 to 3 minutes per side for additional browning. 5. Let the turkey breast rest for 15 minutes before cutting.

Grilled Turkey Drumsticks

Prep Time: 10 minutes | Cook Time: 45 minutes | Serves: 4

2 turkey drumsticks
2 tablespoons olive oil

Poultry Rub

1. To install grill grate, position it flat on top of the heating element so it sits in place, then close hood. Use pellet scoop to pour pellets into smoke box until filled to top. 2. Select GRILL. Select WOODFIRE FLAVOR. Set grill temperature to LO. Set the time to 45 minutes. Select START/STOP to begin preheating. 3. Rub the drumsticks with the olive oil and season with the rub to taste. 4. When unit beeps to signify it has preheated and ADD FOOD displays, open hood and place the drumsticks on the grill grate. Close hood and grill for 45 minutes. 5. Remove the drumsticks from the grill and serve immediately.

Easy Grilled Whole Chicken

Prep Time: 5 minutes | Cook Time: 40 minutes | Serves: 4

1 (4- to 5-pound) whole chicken
Kosher salt

Vegetable oil, for coating the chicken
Freshly ground black pepper

1. Season the chicken generously with salt. Refrigerate overnight. 2. Pat the chicken dry. 3. Lightly coat the chicken with vegetable oil. 4. To install grill grate, position it flat on top of the heating element so it sits in place, then close hood. Use pellet scoop to pour pellets into smoke box until filled to top. 5. Select GRILL. Select WOODFIRE FLAVOR. Set grill temperature to HI. Set the time to 40 minutes. Select START/STOP to begin preheating. 6. When unit beeps to signify it has preheated and ADD FOOD displays, open hood and place chicken breast-side up on the grill grate. Close hood and grill for 40 minutes, flipping halfway through. 7. Season with pepper. Rest for 10 minutes. Carve off the breasts, thighs, legs, and wings; cut the breasts into slices and serve.

Teriyaki Chicken Wings

Prep Time: 10 minutes | Cook Time: 30 minutes | Serves: 4

3 to 4 pounds whole chicken wings, cut into 2 pieces at the joint, tips removed and discarded
1 cup teriyaki sauce, divided
2 tablespoons sesame seeds
2 scallions, green and white parts, sliced

1. To install the grill grate, position it flat on top of the heating element so it sits in place. 2. Select the ROAST function. Adjust the temperature to 375°F and time to 30 minutes. Select START/STOP to begin preheating. 3. When preheating is complete, open the hood. Oil the grill grate, then place the wings on the grate. Once the hood is closed, cooking will begin and the timer will begin counting down, turning and basting with ½ cup of teriyaki sauce every 5 minutes, until the wings reach an internal temperature of 165°F. 4. Transfer the roasted wings to a large bowl. Add the remaining ½ cup of teriyaki sauce and toss the wings until well coated. Serve immediately, sprinkling a bit of scallion and sesame seed onto each serving.

Marinated Isan-Style Chicken Legs

Prep Time: 10 minutes | Cook Time: 16 minutes | Serves: 6

16 garlic cloves, chopped
1 (4-inch) piece lemongrass, tender inner parts only, finely chopped
¼ cup finely chopped fresh cilantro stems
¼ cup packed light brown sugar
4 teaspoons freshly ground black pepper
4 teaspoons turmeric
6 tablespoons fish sauce
¼ cup water
6 chicken legs (with thighs attached)

1. Put the garlic, lemongrass, cilantro stems, sugar, pepper, turmeric, fish sauce, and water in the bowl of a food processor. Pulse until thoroughly combined. Transfer to a large bowl. 2. Add the chicken; toss until thoroughly coated. Refrigerate overnight. 3. To install the grill grate, position it flat on top of the heating element so it sits in place. 4. Select the ROAST function. Adjust the temperature to 400°F and time to 16 minutes. Select START/STOP to begin preheating. 5. When preheating is complete, open the hood and place the chicken skin-side down on the grill grate. Once the hood is closed, cooking will begin and the timer will begin counting down. Roast until grill marks appear and an instant-read thermometer inserted into the thigh without touching the bone registers 160°F. Serve immediately.

Chapter 4 Fish and Seafood Recipes

Smoked Salmon Candy

Prep Time: 20 minutes | Cook Time: 3 hours | Serves: 8

2¼ cups brown sugar
1½ cups kosher salt

5 pounds skin-on salmon, cut into 1½-inch strips
1¼ cups real maple syrup

1. In a medium bowl, combine the brown sugar and salt. Fill a large glass dish or resealable plastic container ¼ inch deep with the mixture. Place the strips, skin-side down, into the mixture. Spread them out a little, as the salmon will need room to cure. If you need to build another layer, repeat the process with ¼ inch of the curing mixture between the layers. Cover and refrigerate for 2 hours. 2. Remove the fish, rinse it off under cold water, and blot dry with paper towels. Place the strips in a clean dish or pan and let them dry in the refrigerator for 24 hours uncovered. 3. To install the grill grate, position it flat on top of the heating element so it sits in place. 4. Place the salmon strips on the grill grate lengthwise, then close the hood. 5. Use the pellet scoop to pour pellets into the smoke box until filled to the top. Select SMOKER. Set grill temperature to 200°F and time to 1 hour. Select START/STOP to begin cooking. Go no higher. Smoke the fish for 3 to 4 hours total, depending on thickness and desired texture. Every 90 minutes, brush the salmon with the maple syrup. 6. Once cooked, the candied salmon will have a deep color with a shiny finish. Remove from the smoker and place onto cooling racks for 1 hour before serving or eating. Store in the refrigerator or freezer in a vacuum-sealed bag.

Mustard-Smoked Salmon Steaks

Prep Time: 20 minutes | Cook Time: 1 hour | Serves: 4

2 tablespoons olive oil
2 tablespoons Dijon mustard
2 teaspoons freshly ground black pepper

1 teaspoon sea salt
2 garlic cloves, minced
4 salmon steaks

1. In a small bowl, combine the olive oil, mustard, black pepper, salt, and garlic. Spoon about 1 tablespoon of the mixture onto each salmon steak. Gently work it onto both sides of the steak. 2. To install the grill grate, position it flat on top of the heating element so it sits in place. 3. Place the salmon steaks on the grill grate, then close the hood. 4. Use the pellet scoop to pour pellets into the smoke box until filled to the top. Select SMOKER. Set grill temperature to 250°F and time to 1 hour. Select START/STOP to begin cooking. 5. Once cooked, remove from the smoker and serve.

Lemon Crab Cakes with Remoulade Sauce

Prep Time: 30 minutes | Cook Time: 28 minutes | Serves: 4

For the Remoulade Sauce:
2 cups mayonnaise
½ cup dill pickles, diced
½ cup bread-and-butter pickles, diced
1 shallot, diced
2 tablespoons capers, roughly chopped
2 tablespoons fresh flat-leaf parsley leaves, very thinly sliced

1 tablespoon Dijon mustard
Grated zest of 1 lemon, plus juice of 1 lemon
1 teaspoon paprika
Flaked sea salt
Freshly ground black pepper

For the Crab Cakes:
4 tablespoons unsalted butter
12 ounces lump crabmeat
¼ cup mayonnaise, lightly whipped
2 scallions, trimmed and finely sliced on the bias
1 large egg
½ cup bread crumbs, plus more as necessary to adjust the texture
1 tablespoon fresh flat-leaf parsley leaves

1 teaspoon Dijon mustard
1 teaspoon Worcestershire sauce
Grated zest of 1 lemon, plus juice of 1 lemon, plus more lemon wedges, for serving
Flaked sea salt
Freshly ground black pepper

To make the remoulade sauce: 1. In a medium bowl, gently fold together the mayonnaise, dill pickles, bread-and-butter pickles, shallot, capers, parsley, mustard, lemon zest, lemon juice, and paprika. Taste and season with salt and pepper. 2. Refrigerate until needed. Taste again and season with salt and pepper, as needed.

To make the crab cakes: 1. Melt half the butter in the microwave and add to a baking pan. 2. In a large bowl, gently fold together the crabmeat, mayonnaise, remaining butter, scallions, egg, bread crumbs, parsley, mustard, Worcestershire sauce, lemon zest, and lemon juice. Season with salt and pepper. Divide the mixture into 4 or 8 portions, depending on the size of cakes you prefer. Gently press and form each portion into a patty. Season with salt and pepper. 3. Place the small crab cakes in the baking pan. 4. To install the grill grate, position it flat on top of the heating element so it sits in place. 5. Place the baking pan on the grill grate, then close the hood. 6. Use the pellet scoop to pour pellets into the smoke box until filled to the top. Select SMOKER. Set grill temperature to 275°F and time to 14 minutes. Select START/STOP to begin cooking. 7. Then turn the cakes over and smoke for another 14 minutes. 8. Serve topped with the remoulade and lemon wedges on the side.

Fennel-Smoked Salmon

Prep Time: 15 minutes | Cook Time: 1 hour | Serves: 6

4 cups ice-cold water
¼ cup kosher salt
¼ cup brown sugar
2 bay leaves

½ cup chopped fennel
2 tablespoons dried onion
2 teaspoons granulated garlic
2 pounds salmon fillets

1. In a large bowl, combine the water, salt, brown sugar, bay leaves, fennel, dried onion, and granulated garlic. Stir until the salt and sugar are completely dissolved. 2. Place the salmon fillets in a glass baking dish, skin-side down. Pour the brine mixture over top. Cover and refrigerate for 6 to 12 hours. 3. Remove the fillets from the brine, rinse them in cold water, and pat dry with paper towels. 4. Place the fillets on a clean plate or dish. Place them in a cool, well ventilated space or your refrigerator for 4 to 5 hours, uncovered. This will cause the surface of the fish to turn opaque, creating what is known as the pellicle. This layer absorbs smoke better. 5. To install the grill grate, position it flat on top of the heating element so it sits in place. 6. Place the salmon fillets on the grill grate, then close the hood. 7. Use the pellet scoop to pour pellets into the smoke box until filled to the top. Select SMOKER. Set grill temperature to 200°F and time to 1 hour. Select START/STOP to begin cooking. 8. Remove and serve.

Orange Soy-Marinated Tuna Steaks

Prep Time: 20 minutes | Cook Time: 1 hour | Serves: 4

4 (7- to 8-ounce) ahi tuna steaks
½ cup reduced-sodium soy sauce
Juice of 1 navel orange
1 tablespoon mirin or dry sherry
2 tablespoons brown sugar

3 garlic cloves, minced
2 teaspoons grated fresh ginger
1 teaspoon onion powder
1 teaspoon sesame oil
½ teaspoon white pepper

1. Place the tuna steaks into a resealable plastic bag. In a medium bowl, whisk together the soy sauce, orange juice, mirin or sherry, brown sugar, garlic, ginger, onion powder, sesame oil, and white pepper. Pour the mixture over the tuna steaks, making sure they are well coated. Seal the bag and refrigerate for 1 hour. 2. To install the grill grate, position it flat on top of the heating element so it sits in place. 3. Remove the tuna steaks from the marinade and place on the grill grate, then close the hood. 4. Use the pellet scoop to pour pellets into the smoke box until filled to the top. Select SMOKER. Set grill temperature to 225°F and time to 1 hour. Select START/STOP to begin cooking. 5. Remove the steaks from your smoker and let stand for a few minutes before serving.

Grilled Spicy BBQ Shrimp

Prep Time: 10 minutes | Cook Time: 30 minutes | Serves: 4

1-pound jumbo shrimp, peeled and deveined
1 tablespoon olive oil

1 to 2 tablespoons BBQ Dry Rub
Pinch cayenne pepper

1. To install grill grate, position it flat on top of the heating element so it sits in place, then close hood. Use pellet scoop to pour pellets into smoke box until filled to top. 2. Select GRILL. Select WOODFIRE FLAVOR. Set grill temperature to LO. Set the time to 30 minutes. Select START/STOP to begin preheating. 3. In a bowl, toss the shrimp with the olive oil, cayenne pepper and dry rub to taste until the shrimp is coated evenly. 4. When unit beeps to signify it has preheated and ADD FOOD displays, open hood and place the shrimp on the grill grate. Close hood and grill for 30 minutes, flipping halfway through.

Herb Butter Smoked Lobster Tails

Prep Time: 10 minutes | Cook Time: 45 minutes | Serves: 4

4 lobster tails
1½ sticks butter, divided

1 rosemary sprig
1 thyme sprig

1. Arrange the lobster tails in a baking pan with the cut side facing up. Cut one stick of butter into smaller pieces and distribute them around the lobster tails in the pan. Also, add the rosemary and thyme to the pan. 2. To install the grill grate, position it flat on top of the heating element so it sits in place. 3. Place the pan on the grill grate, then close the hood. 4. Use the pellet scoop to pour pellets into the smoke box until filled to the top. Select SMOKER. Set grill temperature to 225°F and time to 45 minutes. Select START/STOP to begin cooking. Spoon the herb butter over the lobster tails a few times as they cook. 5. After the lobster has finished cooking, melt the remaining half stick of butter and serve it alongside the lobster for dipping.

Smoked Halibut and Mushrooms

Prep Time: 15 minutes | Cook Time: 45 minutes | Serves: 4

2 tablespoons extra-virgin olive oil, plus more for garnish
2 tablespoons unsalted butter, melted
4 (8-ounce) Alaskan halibut fillets, trimmed, checked for bones, and skin removed
Flaked sea salt
Freshly ground black pepper

8 oyster mushrooms, trimmed and torn lengthwise
4 chanterelle mushrooms, trimmed and torn lengthwise
4 king mushrooms, trimmed and finely sliced lengthwise
2 thyme sprigs, leaves stripped
2 lemons, quartered

1. Brush the halibut with 2 tablespoons of the olive oil and season it on all sides with salt and pepper. Add the melted butter to a baking pan and gently place the fish in the pan, leaving space between the fillets. 2. To install the grill grate, position it flat on top of the heating element so it sits in place. 3. Place the pan on the grill grate, then close the hood. 4. Use the pellet scoop to pour pellets into the smoke box until filled to the top. Select SMOKER. Set grill temperature to 275°F and time to 15 minutes. Select START/STOP to begin cooking. 5. Combine the oyster mushrooms, chanterelle mushrooms, king mushrooms, and thyme in a bowl and add to the baking pan. Toss to coat in the oil and butter and season with salt and pepper. Smoke for 30 minutes more. Gently toss the mushrooms. 6. Remove the halibut from the smoker and let it rest, uncovered, for 5 minutes. 7. Serve the halibut topped with the mushrooms and a drizzle of olive oil, and with the lemon wedges on the side for squeezing.

Delicious Smoked and Ice Oysters

Prep Time: 20 minutes | Cook Time: 15 minutes | Serves: 2

12 fresh oysters, divided
Grated zest of 2 limes, plus juice of 2 limes
2 mint sprigs, leaves stripped and finely sliced

1 tablespoon finely grated fresh ginger
1 tablespoon wildflower honey
¼ cup champagne or other sparkling white wine

1. Store oysters on ice in the refrigerator. Shuck just before preparing: Find the seam where the shell halves come together. Wearing protective gloves, gently work a knife into the crack, twisting left and right until the shells separate. Free the muscle from the shell using a paring knife. Preserve the juices in their half shell and return them to the ice. 2. In a small bowl, whisk together the lime zest, lime juice, mint, ginger, honey, and champagne. Top the oysters in their shells with the marinade. 3. To install the grill grate, position it flat on top of the heating element so it sits in place. 4. Place 6 oysters on the grill grate, leaving space between them, then close the hood. 5. Use the pellet scoop to pour pellets into the smoke box until filled to the top. Select SMOKER. Set grill temperature to 275°F and time to 15 minutes. Select START/STOP to begin cooking. 6. Serve the remaining 6 raw oysters on a bed of crushed ice and serve the smoked oysters in a cast iron skillet.

Savory Crab Cakes with Spicy Mayo

Prep Time: 20 minutes | Cook Time: 30 minutes | Serves: 4

3 tablespoons olive oil, divided
1 red bell pepper, seeded, stemmed, and diced
1 onion, diced
3 celery stalks, diced
Kosher salt
Freshly ground black pepper
Pinch red pepper flakes
3 garlic cloves, minced

2 tablespoons freshly squeezed lemon juice, divided
1½ tablespoons seafood seasoning, divided
1 pound cooked jumbo lump crabmeat
2 eggs, beaten
1 cup panko bread crumbs
1 cup mayonnaise
A few dashes hot sauce of choice
Lemon wedges, for serving (optional)

1. In a large skillet, heat 1 tablespoon of olive oil over medium-high heat. Once hot, add the bell pepper, onion, celery, and a pinch each of salt, black pepper, and red pepper flakes. Cook for 8 to 10 minutes, stirring occasionally. 2. Add the garlic, 1 tablespoon of lemon juice, and ½ tablespoon of seafood seasoning and cook for 1 minute more. Remove from the heat and set the mixture aside to cool. (Cooling is important because if you add the eggs while it's still hot, the eggs will cook and not bind the crab cakes together properly.) 3. Once the mixture has cooled, add the crabmeat, eggs, and bread crumbs. Gently mix this together and form eight patties with your hands. Place them on a tray or baking sheet and refrigerate for 1 hour. 4. To install grill grate, position it flat on top of the heating element so it sits in place, then close hood. Use pellet scoop to pour pellets into smoke box until filled to top. 5. Select GRILL. Select WOODFIRE FLAVOR. Set grill temperature to HI. Set the time to 20 minutes. Select START/STOP to begin preheating. 6. Drizzle the remaining 2 tablespoons of olive oil into a baking pan. 7. When unit beeps to signify it has preheated and ADD FOOD displays, open hood. and place the crab cakes in the prepared baking pan and place the pan on the grill grate. Close hood and grill for 20 minutes, flipping halfway through. 8. While the crab cakes are cooking, combine the mayonnaise, hot sauce, remaining tablespoon of lemon juice, and remaining tablespoon of seafood seasoning. Serve the crab cakes with the spicy mayo on the side and lemon wedges, if desired.

Flavorful Bacon-Wrapped Salmon

Prep Time: 20 minutes | Cook Time: 40 minutes | Serves: 4

1 tablespoon extra-virgin olive oil
4 tablespoons unsalted butter
4 (8-ounce) Chinook salmon fillets, trimmed
2 rosemary sprigs, leaves stripped and minced

Flaked sea salt
Freshly ground black pepper
12 bacon slices
2 lemons, halved

1. In a skillet over medium heat, pour in the olive oil and add the butter to melt. 2. Season the salmon fillets on all sides with the rosemary, salt, and pepper. 3. Firmly (but not too tightly) wrap each fillet with 3 bacon slices, overlapping them, allowing the ends to be exposed. Roll the prepared fillets in the browned butter. 4. To install the grill grate, position it flat on top of the heating element so it sits in place. 5. Place the food on the grill grate, leaving space between each fillet. Then close the hood. 6. Use the pellet scoop to pour pellets into the smoke box until filled to the top. Select SMOKER. Set grill temperature to 275°F and time to 40 minutes. Select START/STOP to begin cooking. 7. Smoke until the salmon flesh is bright pink and opaque, and the bacon is cooked. 8. Serve with lemon halves for squeezing.

Lemon-Herb Roasted Whole Trout

Prep Time: 10 minutes | Cook Time: 14 minutes | Serves: 4

2 whole trout (about 10 ounces each, cavity completely cleaned)
Kosher salt and freshly ground black pepper
1 tablespoon lemon pepper seasoning
3 garlic cloves, minced

1 lemon, sliced thinly into rounds, plus lemon wedges (optional)
2 dill sprigs
2 thyme sprigs
1 tablespoon olive oil

1. Season the trout with salt, black pepper, and lemon pepper seasoning on the outside and inside of the fish. Stuff each cavity with the lemon slices, garlic, dill, and thyme. Brush olive oil on the outside of each fish. 2. To install the grill grate, position it flat on top of the heating element so it sits in place. 3. Select the ROAST function. Adjust the temperature to 400°F and time to 14 minutes. Select START/STOP to begin preheating. 4. When preheating is complete, open the hood and place the trout on the grill grate. Once the hood is closed, cooking will begin and the timer will begin counting down. 5. When cook time reaches zero, the grill will beep and DONE will appear on the display. Remove food from grill grate. 6. Serve with lemon wedges on the side, (if using).

Grilled Swordfish with Mediterranean Mélange

Prep Time: 10 minutes | Cook Time: 45 minutes | Serves: 6

Karl'S "Fish Bath":
¼ cup (½ stick) unsalted butter
½ cup tamari
½ cup Worcestershire sauce
2 tablespoons toasted sesame oil
1 tablespoon garlic powder
The Mélange:
2 tablespoons olive oil, divided
1 large red onion, cut into slivers
1 cup cremini mushrooms, julienned
½ cup Kalamata olives, pitted and cut into slivers
½ cup Peppadew chile peppers, seeded and cut into strips
1 (13.75-ounce) can artichoke hearts, drained and each heart cut into

1 tablespoon Italian seasoning blend
1 tablespoon cracked black peppercorns
1 teaspoon ground ginger
1 teaspoon dried basil

eighths
¼ cup capers, drained
¼ cup slivered oil-packed sun-dried tomatoes
6 (8-ounce) swordfish steaks
¼ cup crumbled feta cheese or to taste

1. In a small saucepan over medium heat, melt the butter, then add the remaining "fish bath" ingredients and whisk to combine. Cook, stirring, for about 2 minutes. Remove from the heat and let cool. 2. Make the mélange. In a large skillet over medium heat, heat 1 tablespoon of the olive oil, then add the onion and cook until lightly caramelized, about 20 minutes, stirring frequently. Throw in the mushrooms and cook until soft, about 5 minutes. Add the olives, Peppadews, artichokes, capers, and sun-dried tomatoes, drizzle the mixture with the remaining 1 tablespoon olive oil, and cook until everything is heated through, 5 to 10 minutes, stirring every few minutes so nothing sticks. Remove from the heat. Reserve at room temperature if you'll be serving that day or refrigerate in an airtight container for up to 2 days. Rewarm before serving. 3. Brush the fish on both sides with the fish bath. 4. To install grill grate, position it flat on top of the heating element so it sits in place, then close hood. Use pellet scoop to pour pellets into smoke box until filled to top. 5. Select GRILL. Select WOODFIRE FLAVOR. Set grill temperature to HI. Set the time to 8 minutes. Select START/STOP to begin preheating. 6. When unit beeps to signify it has preheated and ADD FOOD displays, open hood and place the fish steaks on the grill grate. Close hood and grill for 8 minutes, flipping halfway through and basting every 2 minutes with the fish bath. 7. Transfer the fish to a platter and cover with the mélange. Sprinkle with the crumbled feta cheese. Serve immediately.

Garlic Lobster Tails with Drawn Butter

Prep Time: 10 minutes | Cook Time: 50 minutes | Serves: 4

1 cup butter
2 tablespoons olive oil
1 tablespoon freshly squeezed lemon juice
3 to 4 garlic cloves, minced

2 teaspoons finely chopped fresh basil
⅛ teaspoon salt
⅛ teaspoon freshly ground black pepper
4 (8- to 10-ounce) lobster tails

1. Melt the butter in a large saucepan over medium-high heat until foam starts to collect on the surface, 4 to 5 minutes. Reduce the heat to low and cook for an additional 8 to 10 minutes, or until the milk solids settle at the bottom of the pan. Pour the butter through a cheesecloth-lined strainer or sieve into a bowl. Cover and set aside. 2. Combine the olive oil, lemon juice, garlic, basil, salt, and black pepper in a small bowl. Set aside. 3. Using kitchen shears, cut the lobster shells on the very top of the tail from the cut end to where the tail fans out. Fold open the shell carefully (it's sharp) to expose the flesh underneath. Lift the meat portion out and set it on top of the shell. Do not remove it completely; you just want to shift its position upward. 4. Brush ¼ of the olive oil–herb mixture onto the exposed meat portion of each lobster tail. 5. To install the grill grate, position it flat on top of the heating element so it sits in place. 6. Place the tails on the grill grate, then close the hood. 7. Use the pellet scoop to pour pellets into the smoke box until filled to the top. Select SMOKER. Set grill temperature to 250°F and time to 40 minutes. Select START/STOP to begin cooking. 8. Once the lobster tails are cooked, remove them from your smoker, and serve with the drawn butter.

Teriyaki Shrimp-Pineapple Skewers

Prep Time: 20 minutes | Cook Time: 30 minutes | Serves: 4

24 large raw shrimp (21 to 25 per pound), thawed if frozen, peeled, and deveined
1 pineapple, trimmed, peeled, quartered lengthwise, cored, and cut into large dice
4 cilantro sprigs, leaves stripped and finely sliced, plus more for garnish
4 garlic cloves, minced
4 scallions, trimmed and finely sliced on a 45-degree angle

¼ cup soy sauce
2 tablespoons fish sauce
Grated zest of 2 limes, plus juice of 2 limes
2 tablespoons dark brown sugar
1 tablespoon finely grated fresh ginger
1 teaspoon sesame oil
Flaked sea salt
Freshly ground black pepper

1. Alternate 3 shrimp with 3 pineapple chunks on each of 8 bamboo skewers that have been soaked in water. 2. In a large bowl, whisk together the cilantro, garlic, scallions, soy sauce, fish sauce, lime zest, lime juice, sugar, ginger, and sesame oil. Transfer to a large food-grade plastic bag and add the skewers. Remove as much air as possible from the bag and seal it. Refrigerate for 4 hours, turning the bag 2 or 3 times. 3. Remove the skewers, reserving the marinade in the refrigerator. 4. To install the grill grate, position it flat on top of the heating element so it sits in place. 5. Place the skewers on the grill grate, then close the hood. 6. Use the pellet scoop to pour pellets into the smoke box until filled to the top. Select SMOKER. Set grill temperature to 275°F and time to 10 minutes. Select START/STOP to begin cooking. 7. Brush the shrimp and pineapple with the reserved marinade. Smoke for about 20 minutes more, until the shrimp are fully cooked, pink, and firm.

Smoked Cod with Citrus Olives

Prep Time: 20 minutes | Cook Time: 40 minutes | Serves: 2

1¼ tablespoons extra-virgin olive oil, divided
1 tablespoon unsalted butter
2 (1-pound) cod fillets, trimmed
Flaked sea salt
Freshly ground black pepper

Grated zest of 1 lemon, plus juice of 1 lemon
2 cups Pinot Grigio
1 cup mixed olives, pitted and halved
1 cayenne chile pepper, stemmed and finely sliced
4 flat-leaf parsley sprigs, finely chopped, plus more for garnish

1. Melt the butter in your microwave and pour into a baking pan. Then add the olive oil to the pan. 2. Season the cod on both sides with salt, pepper, and lemon zest. Place the cod in the pan, flesh-side down. 3. To install the grill grate, position it flat on top of the heating element so it sits in place. 4. Place the pan on the grill grate, then close the hood. 5. Use the pellet scoop to pour pellets into the smoke box until filled to the top. Select SMOKER. Set grill temperature to 275°F and time to 15 minutes. Select START/STOP to begin cooking. Smoke until golden brown. 6. Remove the cod from the pan. Pour the wine to deglaze the pan, scraping up any browned bits from the bottom. Add the olives, the remaining ¼ tablespoon of olive oil, and the chile pepper. Taste and season with salt and pepper, as needed. 7. Smoke the pan sauce for 15 minutes more. 8. Return the cod to the pan, flesh-side up. Smoke for about 10 minutes more, until the fish is fully cooked. 9. Top with parsley. Serve in a shallow bowl with the wine and olive sauce and a squeeze of fresh lemon juice.

Buttered Crab Clusters

Prep Time: 10 minutes | Cook Time: 30 minutes | Serves: 4

1 cup melted butter
1 teaspoon salt
1 teaspoon freshly ground black pepper
½ tablespoon ground coriander

2 teaspoons dried oregano
1 teaspoon garlic powder
2 to 3 pounds snow crab clusters

1. Combine the butter, salt, pepper, coriander, oregano, and garlic powder in a large saucepan over low heat. Stir until melted through, then remove from heat and cover to keep warm. 2. Dip the ends of the crab clusters into the butter sauce. 3. To install the grill grate, position it flat on top of the heating element so it sits in place. 4. Place the crab clusters on the grill grate, then close the hood. 5. Use the pellet scoop to pour pellets into the smoke box until filled to the top. Select SMOKER. Set grill temperature to 225°F and time to 25 minutes. Select START/STOP to begin cooking, basting the clusters with the butter sauce every 10 minutes. The shells should be bright in color and the meat should be opaque white. 6. Remove from the smoker and serve hot, or place on ice and serve cold.

Easy Smoked Oysters

Prep Time: 30 minutes | Cook Time: 1 hour | Serves: 6

40 fresh oysters in the shell
1 cup dry white wine

1 cup water
¼ cup good-quality olive oil

1. Rinse the oysters in cold water. In a large pot, bring the wine and water to a boil. Add the oysters in small batches to the boiling liquid. Remove the oysters as they open. Any oyster that doesn't open in 3 minutes should be discarded. 2. Once all the oysters are open, strain the boiling liquid through a paper towel, coffee filter, or cheesecloth, and reserve. 3. With a knife, cut each oyster from the shell and drop it into the liquid. Allow them to soak for 20 minutes. 4. To install the grill grate, position it flat on top of the heating element so it sits in place. 5. Place the oysters on the grill grate, then close the hood. 6. Use the pellet scoop to pour pellets into the smoke box until filled to the top. Select SMOKER. Set grill temperature to 175°F and time to 1 hour. Select START/STOP to begin cooking. 7. Remove the oysters from the smoker, toss with the olive oil, and enjoy.

Smoked Shrimp & Baguette Slices

Prep Time: 20 minutes | Cook Time: 30 minutes | Serves: 4

2 tablespoons extra-virgin olive oil, plus more for brushing
2 tablespoons unsalted butter
1 baguette loaf, cut into ½-inch-thick slices on an angle
Flaked sea salt
Freshly ground black pepper

4 garlic cloves, finely sliced
4 rosemary sprigs
2 pounds shrimp, shelled, deveined, rinsed, and patted dry with a paper towel
Grated zest of 1 lemon, plus juice of 1 lemon

1. To install the grill grate, position it flat on top of the heating element so it sits in place. 2. Brush the baguette slices with olive oil, season with salt and pepper, and arrange them on one side of the grill grate with space between each slice. 3. Melt the butter in your microwave and pour into a small baking pan. Then add the olive oil to the pan. Add the garlic and rosemary. Toss to coat with the oil and butter, season with salt and pepper. Then placed the pan on the other side of the grill grate. 4. Use the pellet scoop to pour pellets into the smoke box until filled to the top. Select SMOKER. Set grill temperature to 275°F and time to 10 minutes. Select START/STOP to begin cooking. 5. After 15 minutes, remove the baguette slices to a serving plate. Add the shrimp and lemon zest to the pan. Toss to coat and season with salt and pepper. Smoke for about 20 minutes, flipping them halfway through. 6. Remove and discard the rosemary. Drizzle the shrimp with lemon juice. Serve with the smoked baguette slices.

Lemony Walnut Salmon

Prep Time: 20 minutes | Cook Time: 25 minutes | Serves: 4

4 (8-ounce) salmon fillets, trimmed, skin removed, and checked for bones
Flaked sea salt
Freshly ground black pepper

Grated zest of 2 lemons, plus juice of 2 lemons, plus 1 lemon, quartered, for serving
1 cup walnuts, finely chopped
1 cup pure maple syrup

1. Season the salmon fillets on both sides with salt and pepper. Top each with lemon zest. 2. On a piece of parchment paper, arrange the chopped walnuts. 3. Brush each fillet with maple syrup and press the fillets into the walnuts. Place the fillets in a baking pan and drizzle with lemon juice. 4. To install the grill grate, position it flat on top of the heating element so it sits in place. 5. Place the pan on the grill grate, then close the hood. 6. Use the pellet scoop to pour pellets into the smoke box until filled to the top. Select SMOKER. Set grill temperature to 275°F and time to 25 minutes. Select START/STOP to begin cooking. Smoke until the salmon is lightly browned and crispy. 7. Serve with lemon wedges for squeezing.

Smoked Peppercorn Littleneck Clams

Prep Time: 20 minutes | Cook Time: 35 minutes | Serves: 4

2 shallots, very thinly sliced
2 flat-leaf parsley sprigs
2 fresh bay leaves
1 cup water
1 cup vodka

10 peppercorns, whole
Flaked sea salt
Freshly ground black pepper
10 pounds littleneck clams, rinsed twice (note: discard any clams that do not close when tapped—see tip)

1. In a large bowl, stir together the shallots, parsley, bay leaves, water, vodka, and peppercorns. Add the mixture to a cast iron pan. Season with salt and pepper. 2. To install the grill grate, position it flat on top of the heating element so it sits in place. 3. Place the pan on the grill grate, then close the hood. 4. Use the pellet scoop to pour pellets into the smoke box until filled to the top. Select SMOKER. Set grill temperature to 275°F and time to 20 minutes. Select START/STOP to begin cooking, stirring occasionally. 5. Add the clams to the pan, cover the pan, and smoke for 8 to 10 minutes, until the clams open. Then smoke the clams for 4 to 5 minutes more. Discard any clams that have not opened. 6. Serve the clams with the sauce. Taste and season with salt and pepper.

Lemon Herb-Grilled Whole Trout

Prep Time: 10 minutes | Cook Time: 10 minutes | Serves: 4

4 small whole rainbow, golden, or mountain trout, heads removed, scaled, and gutted
½ cup mayonnaise
8 sprigs fresh thyme
8 sprigs fresh oregano

4 sprigs fresh rosemary
8 (¼-inch-thick) lemon slices
2 teaspoons chopped garlic (optional)
Extra-virgin olive oil, as needed

1. Coat the outside of each trout with the mayonnaise. In the body cavity of each trout, stuff 2 thyme sprigs, 2 oregano sprigs, 1 rosemary sprig, and 2 lemon slices. Add a little garlic if you like. Refrigerate until ready to grill. 2. To install grill grate, position it flat on top of the heating element so it sits in place, then close hood. Use pellet scoop to pour pellets into smoke box until filled to top. 3. Select GRILL. Select WOODFIRE FLAVOR. Set grill temperature to HI. Set the time to 10 minutes. Select START/STOP to begin preheating. 4. When unit beeps to signify it has preheated and ADD FOOD displays, open hood and place the trout on the grill grate. Close hood and grill for 10 minutes, flipping halfway through. To check doneness, take a cake tester and push it into the thickest part of the fish. Remove the tester and touch it to your lip. If it is warm, the fish should be done. 5. Transfer the trout to a platter and let them rest for 5 minutes. Serve with a drizzle of first-rate extra-virgin olive oil.

Grilled Salmon with Chermoula

Prep Time: 5 minutes | Cook Time: 3 minutes | Serves: 4

4 (3- to 4-ounce) skin-on salmon fillets
Kosher salt

Vegetable oil, for coating the fillets
¼ cup chermoula

1. Pat the salmon dry. Season with salt. Lightly coat with oil. 2. To install grill grate, position it flat on top of the heating element so it sits in place, then close hood. Use pellet scoop to pour pellets into smoke box until filled to top. 3. Select GRILL. Select WOODFIRE FLAVOR. Set grill temperature to HI. Set the time to 2 minutes. Select START/STOP to begin preheating. 4. When unit beeps to signify it has preheated and ADD FOOD displays, open hood and place the salmon skin-side down on the grill grate. Close hood and grill for 2 minutes or until char marks appear and the skin is crisp. 5. Flip and cook the other side for 30 seconds to 1 minute (the center should remain slightly pink). Serve immediately with the chermoula.

Spicy Shrimp Tostadas

Prep Time: 10 minutes | Cook Time: 4 minutes | Serves: 4

1 pound 16/20 shrimp, peeled and deveined
1 teaspoon vegetable oil
1 teaspoon sweet paprika
1 teaspoon ground cumin
¼ teaspoon cayenne pepper
Kosher salt

4 corn tortillas
½ cup charred tomatillo salsa
1 medium tomato, finely diced
Finely diced red onion, for serving
Chopped fresh cilantro, for serving
1 avocado, peeled, pitted, and sliced

1. Pat the shrimp dry. In a large bowl, toss the shrimp with the oil, paprika, cumin, and cayenne. Season with salt. 2. To install grill grate, position it flat on top of the heating element so it sits in place, then close hood. Use pellet scoop to pour pellets into smoke box until filled to top. 3. Select GRILL. Select WOODFIRE FLAVOR. Set grill temperature to HI. Set the time to 4 minutes. Select START/STOP to begin preheating. 4. When unit beeps to signify it has preheated and ADD FOOD displays, open hood and place the shrimp and tortillas on the grill grate. Close hood and grill for 4 minutes or until the shrimp are opaque and the tortillas are crisp. 5. Divide the shrimp among the tostadas. Top with the salsa, tomato, onion, cilantro, and avocado. Serve immediately.

Chapter 5 Beef Recipes

Savory Brisket

Prep Time: 15 minutes | Cook Time: 4 hours and 15 minutes | Serves: 8

1 (5- to 6-pound) brisket flat
2 tablespoons coarse salt

1 tablespoon freshly ground black pepper
¼ cup beef broth

1. Trim any loose pieces of meat or fat from the brisket. Season all surfaces evenly with salt and pepper. 2. To install the grill grate, position it flat on top of the heating element so it sits in place. 3. Place the brisket on the grill grate, then close the hood. 4. Use the pellet scoop to pour pellets into the smoke box until filled to the top. Select SMOKER. Set grill temperature to 225°F and time to 3 hours. Select START/STOP to begin cooking. 5. Remove the brisket from the smoker and place it on a large sheet of aluminum foil. Pour the beef broth over top of the brisket and fold up the sides of the foil, sealing the brisket tightly. Return the wrapped brisket to the smoker. 6. Continue cooking for 1 to 2 hours, or until the internal temperature of the brisket reaches 190°F. Remove from the foil and return to the smoker for an additional 15 to 20 minutes, or until the internal temperature reaches 195° to 200°F. 7. Remove the brisket from the smoker, cover loosely with foil, and let the brisket rest for 15 to 20 minutes. Carve against the grain and serve.

Grilled Filet Roast with Green Peppercorn Gravy

Prep Time: 15 minutes | Cook Time: 16 minutes | Serves: 4

1 (14.5-ounce) can beef broth
⅓ cup red wine
2 garlic cloves, peeled
1 small shallot, cut into ¼-inch slices
1 tablespoon green peppercorns
1 tablespoon black peppercorns

½ teaspoon browning sauce or Worcestershire sauce
½ cup water
2 tablespoons cornstarch
1 (2- to 3-pound) whole filet roast
1 teaspoon salt
1 teaspoon black pepper

1. Make the gravy. In a small saucepan over high heat, combine the beef broth, red wine, garlic, shallot, green peppercorns, and black peppercorns. Bring to a boil. Reduce the heat and simmer the gravy for 3 to 5 minutes. Strain the gravy through a fine-mesh sieve set over the saucepan. Discard the solids. Stir in the browning sauce. In a small bowl, whisk together the water and cornstarch. Place the saucepan over high heat and bring the gravy to a boil. Whisk in the cornstarch slurry and cook for 2 minutes, whisking constantly. Cover the pan, turn off the heat, and reserve for later. 2. Season. Generously season the filet roast with salt and pepper. Cover and let rest at room temperature for 30 minutes. 3. To install grill grate, position it flat on top of the heating element so it sits in place, then close hood. Use pellet scoop to pour pellets into smoke box until filled to top. 4. Select GRILL. Select WOODFIRE FLAVOR. Set grill temperature to HI. Set the time to 16 minutes. Select START/STOP to begin preheating. 5. When unit beeps to signify it has preheated and ADD FOOD displays, open hood and place the filet roast on the grill grate. Close hood and grill for 16 minutes, flipping halfway through. 6. Let the beef rest for 10 minutes. Meanwhile, warm the gravy. Cut the beef into ½-inch-thick slices. Drizzle the hot peppercorn gravy over the sliced meat and serve.

Herbed Rib Roast

Prep Time: 10 minutes | Cook Time: 4 hours | Serves: 10

1 bone-in standing rib roast (about 6 pounds), trimmed of excess fat
6 large cloves garlic, peeled
2 tablespoons fresh rosemary leaves
2 tablespoons fresh thyme leaves

Kosher salt and freshly ground black pepper
3 tablespoons coarse-grain Dijon mustard
3 tablespoons olive oil
Prepared horseradish sauce

1. At least 1 hour before you're ready to begin cooking, remove the roast from the refrigerator. In a food processor or mortar, combine the garlic, rosemary, thyme, and 2 teaspoons each salt and pepper. Pulse to finely mince or crush with a pestle. Add the mustard and pulse or mix to combine. Slowly add the oil with the food processor running or slowly mix in with the pestle until a paste forms. Smear the paste evenly over the entire surface of the roast. For a more intense herb flavor, let the roast sit at room temperature for 2 hours or wrap and refrigerate overnight. 2. Place the roast, bone side down, on a baking pan. 3. To install the grill grate, position it flat on top of the heating element so it sits in place. 4. Place the pan on the grill grate, then close the hood. 5. Use the pellet scoop to pour pellets into the smoke box until filled to the top. Select SMOKER. Set grill temperature to 225°F and time to 4 hours. Select START/STOP to begin cooking. Check after 2½ hours. 6. Transfer the roast to a cutting board, tent with foil, and let rest for at least 30 minutes to let the juices settle. If you wish, make a quick pan gravy out of the drippings. Carve the meat into thin slices and arrange on a warm platter. Serve at once with horseradish sauce and the gravy. 7. Making Gravy: Pour all the accumulated fat and meat juice into a fat separator. Return 2 tablespoons of fat to the pan and discard the rest of it, leaving behind the meat juices. Add enough beef broth to the meat juices to equal 2 cups. Place the pan over medium heat over two burners of your stove. Throw in some chopped shallots and sauté quickly until softened. Add 2 tablespoons superfine flour or cake flour, stir into the fat, and cook for 2 to 3 minutes, stirring. Whisk in the broth. Add a thyme sprig and cook for about 5 minutes. If the gravy begins to get too thick, add more broth. When the gravy has thickened to your liking, gild the lily. Swirl in 2 to 4 tablespoons unsalted butter, 1 tablespoon at a time. Want to really crank this up? Use a combination of unsalted butter and truffle butter. Keep warm over low heat until you serve the roast.

Korean-Style Barbecue Short Ribs

Prep Time: 20 minutes | Cook Time: 10 minutes | Serves: 4

4 pounds boneless beef short ribs
1 cup packed light brown sugar
½ cup soy sauce
⅓ cup water
¼ cup mirin (rice wine)

1 small onion, minced
1 small pear, grated
¼ cup minced garlic
2 tablespoons sesame oil
¼ teaspoon black pepper

1. Cut the beef. Using a sharp knife, cut the beef lengthwise into ¼-inch strips. 2. Marinate. In a medium bowl, whisk the brown sugar, soy sauce, water, mirin, onion, pear, garlic, sesame oil, and pepper until combined. Put the beef in a gallon-size resealable bag and pour the marinade over it. Seal the bag, removing all the air. Refrigerate to marinate for 1 to 4 hours. 3. To install grill grate, position it flat on top of the heating element so it sits in place, then close hood. Use pellet scoop to pour pellets into smoke box until filled to top. 4. Select GRILL. Select WOODFIRE FLAVOR. Set grill temperature to HI. Set the time to 10 minutes. Select START/STOP to begin preheating. 5. When unit beeps to signify it has preheated and ADD FOOD displays, open hood and remove the short ribs from the marinade and place them on the grill grate. Close hood and grill for 10 minutes, flipping halfway through. 6. Let the beef rest for 5 minutes, then serve immediately.

Smoky Spicy Tri-Tip

Prep Time: 20 minutes | Cook Time: 2 hours | Serves: 6

1 (4- to 5-pound) tri-tip roast
2 tablespoons brown sugar
1½ teaspoons smoked paprika
1½ teaspoons kosher salt
1 teaspoon onion powder

1 teaspoon ancho chile powder
½ teaspoon granulated garlic
½ teaspoon freshly ground black pepper
½ teaspoon cayenne pepper

1. Trim any excess fat from the roast's surface. In a small bowl, combine the brown sugar, smoked paprika, salt, onion powder, chile powder, granulated garlic, black pepper, and cayenne pepper. Apply the rub to the meat and let it stand at room temperature for 15 minutes. 2. To install the grill grate, position it flat on top of the heating element so it sits in place. 3. Place the roast on the grill grate, then close the hood. 4. Use the pellet scoop to pour pellets into the smoke box until filled to the top. Select SMOKER. Set grill temperature to 225°F and time to 2 hours. Select START/STOP to begin cooking. 5. When cooking is complete, remove the tri-tip and transfer to a cutting board, then tent with aluminum foil. Let it rest for 10 to 15 minutes before carving.

Smoked Chili Tri-tip

Prep Time: 10 minutes | Cook Time: 2 hours | Serves: 8

1 tri-tip roast (3 to 4 pounds)
1 tablespoon chili powder
1 teaspoon garlic salt

Copious amounts of freshly ground black pepper
Your favorite fresh salsa and pinto beans cooked with bacon for serving

1. At least 1 hour before cooking, remove the roast from the refrigerator. Season all sides with the chili powder, garlic salt, and lots and lots of black pepper. 2. To install the grill grate, position it flat on top of the heating element so it sits in place. 3. Place the roast on the grill grate, then close the hood. 4. Use the pellet scoop to pour pellets into the smoke box until filled to the top. Select SMOKER. Set grill temperature to 225°F and time to 2 hours. Select START/STOP to begin cooking. 5. Transfer the cooked roast to a cutting board, tent with aluminum foil, and let rest for 15 minutes. Slice very thinly against the grain. Arrange on a platter and pour any accumulated juice over the top. Serve with salsa and pinto beans.

Hot Smoked Beef Short Ribs

Prep Time: 25 minutes | Cook Time: 4 hours | Serves: 4

8 (3-ounce) English cut bone-in beef short ribs
3 tablespoons vinegar-based hot sauce
2 tablespoons kosher salt

2 tablespoons freshly ground black pepper
1 tablespoon granulated garlic

1. Brush the ribs all over with the hot sauce and then season with the salt, pepper, and garlic. 2. To install the grill grate, position it flat on top of the heating element so it sits in place. 3. Place the ribs on the grill grate, then close the hood. 4. Use the pellet scoop to pour pellets into the smoke box until filled to the top. Select SMOKER. Set grill temperature to 325°F and time to 4 hours. Select START/STOP to begin cooking. 5. When cooking is complete, remove the ribs from the grill, cover loosely with aluminum foil, and let rest for 20 minutes before serving.

Grilled Beef Fajita Salad

Prep Time: 20 minutes | Cook Time: 15 minutes | Serves: 4

For the Dressing:
2 bunches fresh cilantro
1 garlic clove, minced
¼ cup freshly squeezed lime juice
2 teaspoons honey

½ teaspoon ground cumin
½ teaspoon kosher salt
½ cup extra-virgin olive oil

For the Salad:
2 tablespoons canola oil
1-pound skirt steak
2 teaspoons kosher salt, divided
2 teaspoons freshly ground black pepper, divided
2 romaine lettuce hearts, halved lengthwise

1 red, yellow, or orange bell pepper, cut into ½-inch strips
1 red onion, cut into ½-inch-wide strips
2 tablespoons olive oil
2 avocados, halved and pitted

1. In a food processor, combine the cilantro, garlic, lime juice, honey, cumin, salt, and olive oil. Pulse until smooth and creamy. Transfer the dressing to a serving container. 2. To install grill grate, position it flat on top of the heating element so it sits in place. Lightly grease the baking pan with the canola oil and close hood. Use pellet scoop to pour pellets into smoke box until filled to top. 3. Select GRILL. Select WOODFIRE FLAVOR. Set grill temperature to HI. Set the time to 5 minutes. Select START/STOP to begin preheating. 4. Season the skirt steak with 1 teaspoon of salt and 1 teaspoon of pepper. 5. Lightly drizzle the romaine, bell pepper, and onion with 1½ tablespoons of olive oil. Rub the flesh side of the avocados with the remaining ½ tablespoon of olive oil. Season the vegetables with the remaining 1 teaspoon of salt and 1 teaspoon of pepper. 6. When unit beeps to signify it has preheated and ADD FOOD displays, open hood and place the onion and bell pepper in one side of the hot grill grate. Then place the skirt steak on the grill grate. Close hood and grill for 5 minutes. 7. Flip the steak, then stir the vegetables. Cook the steak for 5 minutes more, until a char forms on the steak or the internal temperature reaches 130°F. Remove the steak from the grill, cover loosely with aluminum foil, and let it rest. 8. Place the romaine and the avocado, cut-side down, directly on the grill. Cook for 5 minutes, or until grill marks appear. Remove the vegetables from the grill. Chop the romaine and avocado. 9. Slice the skirt steak thinly against the grain into strips. Use a tablespoon to scoop the avocado out of its skin, maintaining its shape, then slice it. 10. In a large bowl, toss together the romaine, avocado, bell pepper, and onion. Top the salad with the steak strips and serve with the dressing on the side.

Simple Smoked Beef Brisket

Prep Time: 20 minutes | Cook Time: 14 hours | Serves: 14

1 (12- to 14-pound) whole packer beef brisket
¼ cup coarse salt

¼ cup freshly ground black pepper
Butcher paper or aluminum foil

1. Pat the brisket dry with paper towels and place it on a large cutting board, flat-side down. (The point is rounded and thicker, and the flat is larger and thinner.) Using a sharp knife, score the thinnest portion of the brisket. The meat should be a minimum of 1 inch in thickness. Remove large sections of fat from the brisket, including any membrane. 2. In a small bowl, combine the salt and pepper and apply the mixture evenly over the entire surface of the brisket. Set aside, allowing the meat to absorb the salt and pepper. 3. To install the grill grate, position it flat on top of the heating element so it sits in place. 4. Place the brisket on the grill grate, then close the hood. 5. Use the pellet scoop to pour pellets into the smoke box until filled to the top. Select SMOKER. Set grill temperature to 225°F and time to 8 hours. Select START/STOP to begin cooking. 6. Then remove the brisket and wrap it tightly in butcher paper or aluminum foil. Return it to the smoker. 7. When the brisket reaches an internal temperature of around 200°F, it is done. Place it on a large metal tray, then cover it with large, loose sheets of aluminum foil and a thick towel. (Or wrap it tightly in aluminum foil and place in a cooler at room temperature.) 8. Let the brisket rest for 30 minutes to an hour before carving.

Smoked Tri-Tip Roast

Prep Time: 10 minutes | Cook Time: 2 hours | Serves: 4

1½ pounds tri-tip roast

1 batch Espresso Brisket Rub

1. Season the tri-tip roast with the rub. Using your hands, work the rub into the meat. 2. To install the grill grate, position it flat on top of the heating element so it sits in place. 3. Place the roast on the grill grate, then close the hood. 4. Use the pellet scoop to pour pellets into the smoke box until filled to the top. Select SMOKER. Set grill temperature to 180°F and time to 1½ hours. Select START/STOP to begin cooking. Smoke until its internal temperature reaches 140°F. 5. Increase the grill's temperature to 450°F and continue to cook until the roast's internal temperature reaches 145°F, about half an hour. 6. Remove the tri-tip roast from the grill and let it rest 10 to 15 minutes, before slicing and serving.

Mustard Smoked Pulled Beef

Prep Time: 25 minutes | Cook Time: 6 hours | Serves: 8

1 (4-pound) top round roast
2 tablespoons yellow mustard

1 batch Espresso Brisket Rub
½ cup beef broth

1. Coat the top round roast all over with mustard and season it with the rub. Using your hands, work the rub into the meat. 2. To install the grill grate, position it flat on top of the heating element so it sits in place. 3. Place the roast on the grill grate, then close the hood. 4. Use the pellet scoop to pour pellets into the smoke box until filled to the top. Select SMOKER. Set grill temperature to 225°F and time to 4 hours. Select START/STOP to begin cooking. Smoke until its internal temperature reaches 160°F and a dark bark has formed. 5. Pull the roast from the grill and place it on enough aluminum foil to wrap it completely. 6. Increase the grill's temperature to 350°F. 7. Fold in three sides of the foil around the roast and add the beef broth. Fold in the last side, completely enclosing the roast and liquid. Return the wrapped roast to the grill and cook until its internal temperature reaches 195°F. 8. Pull the roast from the grill and place it in a cooler. Cover the cooler and let the roast rest for 1 or 2 hours. 9. Remove the roast from the cooler and unwrap it. Pull apart the beef using just your fingers. Serve immediately.

Delicious Smoked Roast Beef

Prep Time: 10 minutes | Cook Time: 3 hours | Serves: 8

1 (4-pound) eye-of-round roast
1 tablespoon olive oil

4 tablespoons Beef and Game Rub
⅔ cup low-sodium beef broth, warmed

1. Rub the roast all over with the olive oil. Season the roast liberally with the Beef and Game Rub. 2. To install the grill grate, position it flat on top of the heating element so it sits in place. 3. Place the roast on the grill grate, then close the hood. 4. Use the pellet scoop to pour pellets into the smoke box until filled to the top. Select SMOKER. Set grill temperature to 250°F and time to 3 hours. Select START/STOP to begin cooking. 5. After the first hour of cook time, spritz the roast with the warmed beef broth every 30 minutes for the remaining 2 hours. 6. Once cooked, remove and tent the roast with aluminum foil and let rest for 20 minutes. Uncover, slice, and serve.

Garlic Prime Rib

Prep Time: 20 minutes | Cook Time: 4 hours | Serves: 10

1 (6-pound) prime rib roast
1 tablespoon olive oil
8 garlic cloves, minced
1 tablespoon finely minced shallots
2 tablespoons butter, softened

2½ tablespoons Dijon mustard
2 tablespoons coarse salt
1 tablespoon finely chopped fresh rosemary
1 tablespoon finely chopped fresh marjoram
1 tablespoon coarsely ground black pepper

1. Trim any loose pieces of fat or meat from the roast. 2. Heat the olive oil in a small skillet over low heat. Add the garlic and shallots. Sauté for 2 minutes or until slightly translucent, then remove from heat. 3. In a medium bowl, combine the softened butter, Dijon mustard, salt, rosemary, marjoram, and black pepper to make a paste. Add the garlic and shallots and stir to combine. 4. Coat the roast evenly with the seasoning rub. 5. To install the grill grate, position it flat on top of the heating element so it sits in place. 6. Place the roast on the grill grate, then close the hood. 7. Use the pellet scoop to pour pellets into the smoke box until filled to the top. Select SMOKER. Set grill temperature to 250°F and time to 2 hours. Select START/STOP to begin cooking. 8. After 2 hours, rotate the roast for even cooking and continue smoking for another 2 hours, or until the prime rib reaches an internal temperature of 120°F to 125°F (medium-rare). Remove, tent with foil, and let rest for 20 to 30 minutes before carving.

Homemade Barbecue Beef Back Ribs

Prep Time: 15 minutes | Cook Time: 4 hours | Serves: 4

2 racks (6 to 8 bones each or equivalent) beef back ribs
2 tablespoons salt

1 tablespoon black pepper
1 cup Kansas City–Style Barbecue Sauce

1. Generously season the beef ribs with salt and pepper, covering the surface well. 2. To install the grill grate, position it flat on top of the heating element so it sits in place. 3. Lightly oil the grill grate and place the ribs on the grate, then close the hood. 4. Use the pellet scoop to pour pellets into the smoke box until filled to the top. Select SMOKER. Set grill temperature to 325°F and time to 4 hours. Select START/STOP to begin cooking, turning once every hour. The ribs are fully cooked when the meat pulls back from the bones and the meat feels tender (with no resistance) when probed with a metal skewer or meat thermometer. 5. Brush the ribs with barbecue sauce during the last 5 to 10 minutes of cook time, turning every 2 to 3 minutes. 6. Let the ribs rest for 10 to 15 minutes, then cut into individual portions and serve immediately with any remaining barbecue sauce on the side.

Bacon and Mushroom Cheeseburgers

Prep Time: 10 minutes | Cook Time: 20 minutes | Serves: 4

8 bacon slices
8 ounces cremini mushrooms, sliced
Kosher salt
Freshly ground black pepper

2 pounds ground beef
4 Swiss cheese slices
4 kaiser rolls, split
½ cup aioli

1. To install grill grate, position it flat on top of the heating element so it sits in place, then close hood. Use pellet scoop to pour pellets into smoke box until filled to top. 2. Select GRILL. Select WOODFIRE FLAVOR. Set grill temperature to HI. Set the time to 2 minutes. Select START/STOP to begin preheating. 3. When unit beeps to signify it has preheated and ADD FOOD displays, open hood. Put the bacon in a baking pan and place the pan on the grill grate. Close hood and grill for 2 minutes or until browned and crispy around the edges. Transfer to a plate. 4. Add the mushrooms to the pan. Close the hood and cook, stirring once, for 7 to 9 minutes or until browned. Transfer to a plate. Season with salt and pepper. 5. Meanwhile, in a large bowl, season the beef with pepper and 4 teaspoons of salt. Using your hands, mix until just incorporated; form into four 1-inch-thick patties with a slight dimple in the center. 6. Put the burgers on the grill grate. Close the hood and cook, flipping halfway through, for 8 to 10 minutes total for medium, or until an instant-read thermometer inserted into the center registers 135°F. In the last minute of cooking, top the patties with the cheese to melt and place the rolls cut-side down on the grate to toast. 7. Spread the aioli on the buns and assemble the burgers, evenly dividing the bacon and mushrooms among them. Serve right away.

Tangy Red Wine-Braised Short Ribs

Prep Time: 10 minutes | Cook Time: 3 hours | Serves: 4

2 pounds bone-in beef short ribs
Kosher salt
1 teaspoon vegetable oil
1 medium onion, coarsely chopped
3 medium carrots, coarsely chopped

Freshly ground black pepper
2 cups red wine
2 cups low-sodium beef broth
10 fresh thyme sprigs
2 bay leaves

1. Season the beef generously with salt. Refrigerate overnight. 2. Pat the beef dry. 3. To install grill grate, position it flat on top of the heating element so it sits in place. Pour the oil into a baking pan and place on the grill grate, then close hood. Use pellet scoop to pour pellets into smoke box until filled to top. 4. Select GRILL. Select WOODFIRE FLAVOR. Set grill temperature to HI. Set the time to 20 minutes. Select START/STOP to begin preheating. 5. When unit beeps to signify it has preheated and ADD FOOD displays, open hood and place the beef in a single layer in the preheated pan on the grill grate. Close hood and grill for 20 minutes, turning every 5 to 6 minutes. Transfer to a plate. 6. Add the onion and carrots to the pan. Close the hood and cook for 8 to 10 minutes or until softened. Season with salt and pepper. 7. Pour in the wine and broth to deglaze: Close the hood, bring to a boil, and gently scrape the bottom of the pan with a wooden spoon to loosen any browned bits. 8. Add the thyme and bay leaves. Close the hood and cook for 13 to 15 minutes or until the liquid is reduced by half, then add the beef. 9. Reduce the grill temperature to low. 10. Close the hood and cook for 2 hours to 2 hours 30 minutes or until the beef is fork-tender. 11. Rest for 20 minutes before serving.

Tasty Beef Kebabs

Prep Time: 15 minutes | Cook Time: 10 minutes | Serves: 4

⅓ cup red wine vinegar
½ cup olive oil
1 tablespoon paprika
1 tablespoon chopped garlic
1 teaspoon ground cumin

1 teaspoon salt
½ teaspoon black pepper
½ teaspoon ground turmeric
2 pounds beef tenderloin, cut into 1-inch cubes

1. In a medium bowl, whisk the vinegar, olive oil, paprika, garlic, cumin, salt, pepper, and turmeric to combine. Put the beef cubes in a gallon-size resealable bag and pour the marinade over the beef. Seal the bag, removing all the air. Refrigerate to marinate for 1 hour. 2. Remove the beef cubes from the marinade and thread them onto 8 metal skewers. Discard the marinade. 3. To install grill grate, position it flat on top of the heating element so it sits in place, lightly oil the grill grate and close hood. Use pellet scoop to pour pellets into smoke box until filled to top. 4. Select GRILL. Select WOODFIRE FLAVOR. Set grill temperature to HI. Set the time to 10 minutes. Select START/STOP to begin preheating. 5. When unit beeps to signify it has preheated and ADD FOOD displays, open hood and place the beef skewers on the grill grate. Close hood and grill for 10 minutes, turning frequently. Serve immediately while hot.

Juicy Carne Asada

Prep Time: 15 minutes | Cook Time: 10 minutes | Serves: 4

⅓ cup freshly squeezed orange juice
2 garlic cloves, finely chopped
1 teaspoon dried oregano
1 teaspoon chili powder

1 teaspoon ground cumin
2 teaspoons salt
2 pounds beef skirt steak or flap meat, cut into 6- to 8-inch lengths

1. In a medium bowl, whisk the orange juice, garlic, oregano, chili powder, cumin, and salt until combined. Put the skirt steak in a gallon-size resealable bag and pour the marinade over it. Seal the bag, removing all the air. Refrigerate to marinate for 1 to 2 hours. 2. To install grill grate, position it flat on top of the heating element so it sits in place, lightly oil the grill grate and close hood. Use pellet scoop to pour pellets into smoke box until filled to top. 3. Select GRILL. Select WOODFIRE FLAVOR. Set grill temperature to HI. Set the time to 10 minutes. Select START/STOP to begin preheating. 4. When unit beeps to signify it has preheated and ADD FOOD displays, open hood and remove the meat from the marinade and place it on the grill grate. Close hood and grill for 10 minutes, turning every few minutes, until the meat is cooked to medium-rare (130°F to 140°F). 5. Let the meat rest for 5 minutes. Cut the carne asada against the grain into strips and serve immediately.

Honey-Citrus Flank Steak

Prep Time: 15 minutes | Cook Time: 14 minutes | Serves: 4

3 garlic cloves, finely chopped
⅓ cup freshly squeezed lime juice
¼ cup honey
2 tablespoons chopped fresh cilantro

2 tablespoons balsamic vinegar
1 teaspoon ground cumin
1 teaspoon salt
1 (2- to 3-pound) flank steak

1. In a medium bowl, whisk the garlic, lime juice, honey, cilantro, vinegar, cumin, and salt until combined. Put the flank steak in a gallon-size resealable bag and pour the marinade over it. Seal the bag, removing all the air. Refrigerate to marinate for 1 to 4 hours. 2. To install grill grate, position it flat on top of the heating element so it sits in place, lightly oil the grill grate and close hood. Use pellet scoop to pour pellets into smoke box until filled to top. 3. Select GRILL. Select WOODFIRE FLAVOR. Set grill temperature to HI. Set the time to 14 minutes. Select START/STOP to begin preheating. 4. When unit beeps to signify it has preheated and ADD FOOD displays, open hood and remove the steak from the marinade and place it on the grill grate. Discard the marinade. Close hood and grill for 14 minutes, flipping halfway through. 5. Let the meat rest for 5 minutes. Cut the meat against the grain into ½-inch strips and serve immediately.

Garlic Coffee-Rubbed Rib Eye Steaks

Prep Time: 15 minutes | Cook Time: 12 minutes | Serves: 4

3 tablespoons light brown sugar
2 tablespoons freshly ground coffee
2 tablespoons salt
1 tablespoon black pepper

1 tablespoon garlic powder
1½ teaspoons onion powder
4 (1½-inch-thick) boneless rib eye steaks

1. In a small bowl, stir together the brown sugar, coffee, salt, pepper, garlic powder, and onion powder. Evenly sprinkle the rub over each steak until fully coated on all sides. Cover and let rest at room temperature for 30 minutes. 2. To install grill grate, position it flat on top of the heating element so it sits in place, lightly oil the grill grate and close hood. Use pellet scoop to pour pellets into smoke box until filled to top. 3. Select GRILL. Select WOODFIRE FLAVOR. Set grill temperature to HI. Set the time to 12 minutes. Select START/STOP to begin preheating. 4. When unit beeps to signify it has preheated and ADD FOOD displays, open hood and place the steaks on the grill grate. Close hood and grill for 12 minutes, flipping halfway through. 5. Let the steaks rest for 5 minutes, then serve immediately.

Smoked Pulled Beef

Prep Time: 20 minutes | Cook Time: 4 hours | Serves: 4

1 (3-pound) chuck roast
2 tablespoons salt, plus more for seasoning

2 tablespoons black pepper

1. Season the chuck roast with salt and pepper, covering the surface fully. 2. To install the grill grate, position it flat on top of the heating element so it sits in place. 3. Lightly oil the grill grate and place the roast on the grate, then close the hood. 4. Use the pellet scoop to pour pellets into the smoke box until filled to the top. Select SMOKER. Set grill temperature to 325°F and time to 4 hours. Select START/STOP to begin cooking, turning once every hour. 5. The roast is fully cooked when the meat reaches an internal temperature of 180°F and feels tender (with no resistance) when probed with a metal skewer or meat thermometer. 6. Let the roast rest for 10 to 15 minutes. Using two large forks, pull apart the beef. Taste and season with more salt to taste and serve immediately.

Bacon-Wrapped Filet Mignon Steaks

Prep Time: 15 minutes | Cook Time: 8 minutes | Serves: 4

8 tablespoons (1 stick) butter, at room temperature
2 garlic cloves, finely chopped
2 tablespoons finely chopped fresh parsley
¼ teaspoon salt

¼ teaspoon black pepper
4 thick-cut bacon slices
4 (8- to 10-ounce) beef filets

1. Make the compound butter. In a medium bowl, stir together the butter, garlic, parsley, salt, and pepper until thoroughly combined. Place a 12-inch piece of plastic wrap onto a cutting board. Spread the butter evenly in a 2-inch-wide strip in the middle of the plastic wrap. Fold the plastic wrap in half, then tighten into a cylinder shape to refrigerate. 2. Prepare the filets. One at a time, place a bacon slice on a cutting board. Place a filet on the end of the bacon slice. Roll the filet to wrap the bacon firmly around it and pierce a toothpick through the bacon to secure it to the steak. Repeat. 3. To install grill grate, position it flat on top of the heating element so it sits in place, then close hood. Use pellet scoop to pour pellets into smoke box until filled to top. 4. Select GRILL. Select WOODFIRE FLAVOR. Set grill temperature to HI. Set the time to 8 minutes. Select START/STOP to begin preheating. 5. When unit beeps to signify it has preheated and ADD FOOD displays, open hood and place the filets on the grill grate. Close hood and grill for 8 minutes, flipping halfway through. Grill until the steaks are cooked to your preference. 6. Let the filets rest for 2 to 3 minutes. Place ½-inch slice of compound butter, centered, on top of each filet. Serve immediately.

Smoked Juicy Tri-Tip

Prep Time: 20 minutes | Cook Time: 5 hours | Serves: 4

1½ pounds tri-tip roast
Salt
Freshly ground black pepper

2 teaspoons garlic powder
2 teaspoons lemon pepper
½ cup apple juice

1. Season the tri-tip roast with salt, pepper, garlic powder, and lemon pepper. Using your hands, work the seasoning into the meat. 2. To install the grill grate, position it flat on top of the heating element so it sits in place. 3. Place the roast on the grill grate, then close the hood. 4. Use the pellet scoop to pour pellets into the smoke box until filled to the top. Select SMOKER. Set grill temperature to 180°F and time to 4 hours. Select START/STOP to begin cooking. 5. Pull the tri-tip from the grill and place it on enough aluminum foil to wrap it completely. 6. Increase the grill's temperature to 375°F. 7. Fold in three sides of the foil around the roast and add the apple juice. Fold in the last side, completely enclosing the tri-tip and liquid. Return the wrapped tri-tip to the grill and cook for 45 minutes more. 8. Remove the tri-tip roast from the grill and let it rest for 10 to 15 minutes, before unwrapping, slicing, and serving.

Grilled New York Strip Steaks with Herbed Mushrooms

Prep Time: 15 minutes | Cook Time: 15 minutes | Serves: 4

¼ cup black pepper
1½ tablespoons garlic powder
1 tablespoon salt
4 (8- to 10-ounce, 1-inch-thick) boneless New York strip steaks

2 tablespoons olive oil
1 teaspoon fresh or dried thyme leaves
1 teaspoon fresh or dried rosemary leaves
8 ounces button mushrooms, cleaned, stemmed, and thinly sliced

1. Season. In a small bowl, stir together the pepper, garlic powder, and salt until fully blended. Evenly cover each steak with the seasoning so all surfaces are coated. 2. To install grill grate, position it flat on top of the heating element so it sits in place, then close hood. Use pellet scoop to pour pellets into smoke box until filled to top. 3. Select GRILL. Select WOODFIRE FLAVOR. Set grill temperature to HI. Set the time to 10 minutes. Select START/STOP to begin preheating. 4. When unit beeps to signify it has preheated and ADD FOOD displays, open hood and place the steaks on the grill grate. Close hood and grill for 10 minutes, flipping halfway through. Grill until the steaks are cooked to your preference. 5. Let the steaks rest for 10 minutes. 6. Grill the mushrooms. As soon as the steaks begin resting, Combine the olive oil, thyme, rosemary, and mushrooms in a small bowl and place on the grill grate. Grill on HI heat for 5 minutes, until the mushrooms are reduced in size by half. Top each steak with grilled mushrooms and serve.

Chapter 6 Lamb, and Venison Recipes

Spicy Curried Lamb Chops with Yogurt Sauce

Prep Time: 20 minutes | Cook Time: 10 minutes | Serves: 4

Sauce:
½ cup plain whole-milk Greek yogurt
1 tablespoon finely chopped cilantro leaves
2 teaspoons lime juice
1 teaspoon chile-garlic paste

½ garlic clove, minced
¼ teaspoon kosher salt
⅛ teaspoon garam masala

Marinade:
3 tablespoons lime juice
2 tablespoons peeled, finely grated fresh ginger
2 tablespoons extra-virgin olive oil
2 teaspoons Madras curry powder
1 teaspoon smoked paprika

1 teaspoon ground turmeric
1 teaspoon cayenne pepper
1 teaspoon kosher salt
1 teaspoon freshly ground black pepper
8 lamb loin chops, each 1½ inches thick, trimmed

1. In a small bowl, whisk together all the sauce ingredients. Cover and refrigerate until 30 minutes before serving. (The sauce can be made up to 8 hours in advance.) 2. In a separate small bowl, whisk together all the marinade ingredients. Place the lamb chops in a large glass baking dish, pour the marinade over them, and turn the chops to coat evenly. Cover and refrigerate for at least 2 hours or up to 4 hours. Let the chops stand at room temperature for 15 to 30 minutes before grilling. 3. To install grill grate, position it flat on top of the heating element so it sits in place, then close hood. Use pellet scoop to pour pellets into smoke box until filled to top. 4. Select GRILL. Select WOODFIRE FLAVOR. Set grill temperature to HI. Set the time to 10 minutes. Select START/STOP to begin preheating. 5. When unit beeps to signify it has preheated and ADD FOOD displays, remove the chops from the dish and discard the marinade. Open hood and place the lamb chops on the grill grate. Close hood and grill for 10 minutes, flipping halfway through. Remove from the grill and let rest for 3 to 5 minutes. 6. Serve the chops warm, with the yogurt sauce alongside.

Grilled Leg of Lamb with Zucchini Salad

Prep Time: 35 minutes | Cook Time: 26 minutes | Serves: 8

Marinade:
¼ cup extra-virgin olive oil
1 tablespoon finely chopped fresh rosemary leaves
1 tablespoon minced garlic
1 teaspoon kosher salt

½ teaspoon coarse-ground black pepper
1 boneless leg of lamb, 3 to 4 pounds, butterflied, trimmed of fat, and cut into 3 or 4 equal sections

Salad:
12 ounces small zucchini, trimmed and halved lengthwise
1 small red onion, cut into ½-inch-thick slices
Extra-virgin olive oil
8 ounces cherry tomatoes, cut into halves

2 tablespoons pitted, chopped Kalamata olives
2 tablespoons drained, finely chopped oil-packed sun-dried tomatoes
2 tablespoons finely chopped fresh mint leaves
Lemon-Parsley Dressing

1. In a small bowl, whisk together all the marinade ingredients. Put the lamb in a spacious, sealable plastic bag and pour in the marinade. Squeeze out the air from the bag and tightly seal it. Turn the bag to distribute the marinade evenly, place the bag in a bowl, and refrigerate for 2 to 12 hours, turning the bag occasionally. 2. To install grill grate, position it flat on top of the heating element so it sits in place, then close hood. Use pellet scoop to pour pellets into smoke box until filled to top. 3. Select GRILL. Select WOODFIRE FLAVOR. Set grill temperature to LO. Set the time to 6 minutes. Select START/STOP to begin preheating. 4. Brush the zucchini and onion evenly with oil. 5. When unit beeps to signify it has preheated and ADD FOOD displays, open hood and place zucchini and onion on the grill grate. Close hood and grill for 6 minutes, flipping halfway through. 6. Remove from the grill. Let cool slightly, then cut the zucchini on the diagonal into ½-inch-thick slices and chop the onion. 7. In a serving bowl, combine the zucchini, onion, cherry tomatoes, olives, sun-dried tomatoes, and mint. 8. Spoon 3 tablespoons of the dressing over the salad. Toss to coat evenly. Reserve the remaining dressing. 9. Place the lamb pieces on the grill grate. Close the hood and grill on HI for about 20 minutes. Then remove the lamb from the grill and let rest for 5 minutes. 10. Cut the lamb across the grain into thin slices. Spoon the reserved dressing over the meat. Serve warm with the salad.

Rosemary-Garlic Lamb Chops

Prep Time: 10 minutes | Cook Time: 20 minutes | Serves: 4

4 (8-ounce) bone-in lamb chops
2 tablespoons olive oil

1 batch Rosemary-Garlic Lamb Seasoning

1. Rub the lamb chops all over with olive oil and coat them on both sides with the seasoning. 2. To install grill grate, position it flat on top of the heating element so it sits in place, then close hood. Use pellet scoop to pour pellets into smoke box until filled to top. 3. Select GRILL. Select WOODFIRE FLAVOR. Set grill temperature to HI. Set the time to 20 minutes. Select START/STOP to begin preheating. 4. When unit beeps to signify it has preheated and ADD FOOD displays, open hood and place the chops on the grill grate. Close hood and grill for 20 minutes, flipping halfway through. 5. Remove the chops from the grill and serve immediately.

Smoked Rosemary Lamb Chops

Prep Time: 15 minutes | Cook Time: 1½-2 hours | Serves: 4

4½ pounds bone-in lamb chops
2 tablespoons olive oil
Salt

Freshly ground black pepper
1 bunch fresh rosemary

1. Rub the lamb chops all over with olive oil and season on both sides with salt and pepper. 2. To install the grill grate, position it flat on top of the heating element so it sits in place. 3. Spread the rosemary directly on the grill grate, creating a surface area large enough for all the chops to rest on. Place the chops on the rosemary, then close the hood. 4. Use the pellet scoop to pour pellets into the smoke box until filled to the top. Select SMOKER. Set grill temperature to 180°F and time to 1½ hours. Select START/STOP to begin cooking. Smoke until they reach an internal temperature of 135°F. 5. Increase the grill's temperature to 450°F, remove the rosemary, and continue to cook the chops until their internal temperature reaches 145°F, about 30 minutes. 6. Remove the chops from the grill and let them rest for 5 minutes before serving.

Grilled Rosemary-Garlic Lamb Chops

Prep Time: 10 minutes | Cook Time: 30 minutes | Serves: 4

4 (8-ounce) bone-in lamb chops
2 tablespoons olive oil

1 batch Rosemary-Garlic Lamb Seasoning

1. Rub the lamb chops all over with olive oil and coat them on both sides with the seasoning. 2. To install grill grate, position it flat on top of the heating element so it sits in place, then close hood. Use pellet scoop to pour pellets into smoke box until filled to top. 3. Select GRILL. Select WOODFIRE FLAVOR. Set grill temperature to HI. Set the time to 30 minutes. Select START/STOP to begin preheating. 4. When unit beeps to signify it has preheated and ADD FOOD displays, open hood and place the chops on the grill grate. Close hood and grill for 30 minutes, flipping halfway through. Grill until their internal temperature reaches 145°F. Remove the chops from the grill and serve immediately.

Hoisin Sauce-Flavored Lamb Shanks

Prep Time: 25minutes | Cook Time: 2½ hours | Serves: 4

2 (2-pound) lamb shanks
½ teaspoon salt
½ teaspoon freshly ground black pepper
¾ cup hoisin sauce
¾ cup beef broth
¼ cup freshly squeezed orange juice
2 tablespoons brown sugar

1 teaspoon freshly squeezed lemon juice
2 garlic cloves, minced
2 teaspoons grated ginger
1 tablespoon tomato paste
¼ teaspoon white pepper
¼ teaspoon cinnamon
¼ teaspoon red pepper flakes

1. Blot the lamb shanks with paper towels. Using a sharp knife, remove the silver skin around the shank and season with the salt and pepper. 2. To install the grill grate, position it flat on top of the heating element so it sits in place. 3. Place the shanks on the grill grate, then close the hood. 4. Use the pellet scoop to pour pellets into the smoke box until filled to the top. Select SMOKER. Set grill temperature to 250°F and time to 1½ hours. Select START/STOP to begin cooking. Cook until they reach an internal temperature of 165°F. Remove and place onto a cutting board. 5. Increase the temperature to 325°F. 6. Combine the hoisin sauce, beef broth, orange juice, brown sugar, lemon juice, garlic, ginger, tomato paste, white pepper, cinnamon, and red pepper flakes in a medium bowl. 7. Place the shanks in a baking pan. Pour the braising liquid over them and then place the pan or pot back into the smoker, for 2 hours. Add more beef broth if needed. 8. Remove the lamb shanks from the smoker and uncover. Let stand for 10 to 15 minutes. 9. Shred the meat and place it back into the braising liquid, mixing to combine. Serve with your favorite side dish or in tacos with sliced chile peppers and pickled vegetables.

Herbed Rack of Lamb

Prep Time: 10 minutes | Cook Time: 2 hours | Serves: 4

2 tablespoons olive oil
4 garlic cloves, minced
1 tablespoon dried rosemary
1 tablespoon dried thyme

1 tablespoon dried basil
Kosher salt
Freshly ground black pepper
1 (2-pound) rack of lamb

1. In a small bowl, mix together the olive oil, garlic, rosemary, thyme, basil, salt, and pepper. Use your hands to rub this mixture over all sides of the lamb. 2. To install the grill grate, position it flat on top of the heating element so it sits in place. 3. Place the lamb on the grill grate, then close the hood. 4. Use the pellet scoop to pour pellets into the smoke box until filled to the top. Select SMOKER. Set grill temperature to 225°F and time to 2 hours. Select START/STOP to begin cooking. 5. Let it rest for 15 minutes before slicing.

Lamb Cheeseburgers

Prep Time: 20 minutes | Cook Time: 10 minutes | Serves: 4

2 pounds ground lamb
4 teaspoons kosher salt
Freshly ground black pepper
4 kaiser rolls, split

1 cup tzatziki
Sliced red onion, for topping
½ cup crumbled feta cheese, for topping

1. To install grill grate, position it flat on top of the heating element so it sits in place, then close hood. Use pellet scoop to pour pellets into smoke box until filled to top. 2. Select GRILL. Select WOODFIRE FLAVOR. Set grill temperature to HI. Set the time to 10 minutes. Select START/STOP to begin preheating. 3. In the meantime, in a large bowl, blend the lamb with the salt and pepper. Using your hands, combine until just mixed; shape the mixture into four 1-inch-thick patties with a slight indentation in the center. 4. When unit beeps to signify it has preheated and ADD FOOD displays, open hood and place the burgers on the grill grate. Close hood and grill for 10 minutes, flipping halfway through. 5. In the last minute of cooking, place the rolls cut-side down on the grate to toast. 6. Spread the tzatziki on the buns and assemble the burgers, topping them with the onion and feta. Serve immediately.

Herb-Mustard Marinated Leg of Lamb

Prep Time: 10 minutes | Cook Time: 1 to 1½ hours | Serves: 8

1 (4- to 5-pound) boneless or 1 (6- to 8-pound) bone-in leg of lamb
¾ cup vegetable oil
½ cup red wine vinegar
½ cup chopped onion
2 cloves garlic, bruised
2 teaspoons Dijon mustard

2 teaspoons kosher salt
½ teaspoon dried oregano
½ teaspoon dried basil
1 bay leaf
1/8 teaspoon freshly ground black pepper

1. If working with a bone-in leg, have your butcher bone the leg and butterfly it. Place the lamb in a 2½-gallon zip-top plastic bag. 2. In a medium bowl, whisk the oil, vinegar, onion, garlic, mustard, salt, oregano, basil, bay leaf, and pepper together. Add to the bag, seal, and squish the marinade all around to coat the lamb. Refrigerate for 48 hours, turning the bag over occasionally. 3. Remove the lamb from the marinade, reserving the marinade. Pat the lamb dry and let sit at room temperature for about 30 minutes. Bring the marinade to a full boil in a small saucepan over high heat. Reduce the heat slightly and cook for 5 minutes. Remove from the heat and let cool. 4. To install the grill grate, position it flat on top of the heating element so it sits in place. 5. Select the ROAST function. Adjust the temperature to 500°F and time to 10 minutes. Select START/STOP to begin preheating. 6. When preheating is complete, open the hood and place lamb on the grill grate. Once the hood is closed, cooking will begin and the timer will begin counting down, flipping halfway through. 7. When cook time reaches zero, the grill will beep and DONE will appear on the display. Remove food from grill grate. 8. Set the lamb on a rack in a roasting pan and put the pan on the grill. Close the hood and adjust the temperature to 350°F. Roast until the internal temperature at the thickest point of the lamb registers 135° F, about 1 to 1½ hours. 9. Transfer the lamb to a cutting board and let rest for 10 minutes. The lamb will be crusty on the outside and cooked to multiple levels of doneness, from rare to well done. Cut into slices and serve with the reserved marinade, reheated, as a dipping sauce.

Delicious Lamb Kebabs with Lemon-Dill Sauce

Prep Time: 15 minutes | Cook Time: 12 minutes | Serves: 4

2 pounds boneless lamb (shoulder or leg)
10 ounces Greek yogurt
2 tablespoons mayonnaise
2 tablespoons freshly squeezed lemon juice
2 tablespoons chopped fresh dill

1 tablespoon garlic paste
Kosher salt
Freshly ground black pepper
4 to 6 kebab skewers (if using wooden skewers, soak in water for at least 30 minutes to prevent burning)

1. Cut the lamb into 1-inch pieces and place them in a gallon-size plastic bag. 2. To make the lemon-dill sauce, in a bowl, combine the Greek yogurt, mayonnaise, lemon juice, dill, garlic paste, salt, and pepper and stir together. Place 2 to 3 tablespoons of the lemon-dill sauce into the bag with the lamb and massage the bag until the lamb is evenly coated. Marinate in the refrigerator for 2 to 3 hours. 3. To install grill grate, position it flat on top of the heating element so it sits in place, then close hood. Use pellet scoop to pour pellets into smoke box until filled to top. 4. Select GRILL. Select WOODFIRE FLAVOR. Set grill temperature to HI. Set the time to 12 minutes. Select START/STOP to begin preheating. 5. Thread the lamb on the kebab skewers. 6. When unit beeps to signify it has preheated and ADD FOOD displays, open hood and place the kebabs on the grill grate. Close hood and grill for 12 minutes, turning a few times throughout. 7. Remove from the grill and serve the lamb kebabs with the remaining lemon-dill sauce for dipping.

Mustard Curry-Rubbed Leg of Lamb

Prep Time: 10 minutes | Cook Time: 2½ hours | Serves: 12

1 (5- to 6-pound) bone-in leg of lamb
¼ cup Dijon mustard
2 tablespoons curry powder
1 teaspoon garlic powder
1 teaspoon ginger powder

1 teaspoon ground cumin
1 teaspoon ground coriander
Kosher salt
Freshly ground black pepper

1. Brush the leg of lamb with the Dijon mustard on all sides. 2. In a small bowl, mix the curry powder, garlic powder, ginger powder, cumin, coriander, salt, and pepper until evenly combined. Rub the mixture into the Dijon mustard on all sides of the lamb. 3. To install the grill grate, position it flat on top of the heating element so it sits in place. 4. Place the leg of lamb on the grill grate, then close the hood. 5. Use the pellet scoop to pour pellets into the smoke box until filled to the top. Select SMOKER. Set grill temperature to 250°F and time to 2½ hours. Select START/STOP to begin cooking. 6. Let the lamb rest for 20 to 30 minutes before serving.

Savory Lamb Burgers with Basil-Feta Sauce

Prep Time: 15 minutes | Cook Time: 10 minutes | Serves: 4

1½ pounds ground lamb
1 teaspoon garlic powder
1 teaspoon paprika
1 teaspoon ground cumin
Kosher salt
Freshly ground black pepper
Toppings of choice: lettuce, tomato, onions, etc.

6 ounces plain Greek yogurt
2 ounces crumbled feta cheese
5 or 6 basil leaves, chopped
1 tablespoon freshly squeezed lemon juice
4 burger buns

1. In a bowl, combine the garlic powder, cumin, salt, paprika, and pepper. Combine the ingredients using your hands, being cautious not to overmix, and shape the mixture into four patties. 2. In a separate bowl, combine the Greek yogurt, feta, basil, lemon juice, and a pinch each of salt and pepper and stir until evenly mixed, then set aside. 3. To install grill grate, position it flat on top of the heating element so it sits in place, then close hood. Use pellet scoop to pour pellets into smoke box until filled to top. 4. Select GRILL. Select WOODFIRE FLAVOR. Set grill temperature to HI. Set the time to 10 minutes. Select START/STOP to begin preheating. 5. When unit beeps to signify it has preheated and ADD FOOD displays, open hood and place the lamb burgers on the grill grate. Close hood and grill for 10 minutes, flipping halfway through. 6. Toast the burger buns in the grill during the last minute of cooking the burgers. 7. Present the lamb burgers on buns and garnish with the basil-feta sauce, along with any preferred toppings such as lettuce, tomato, or onions, if desired.

Lamb Pita Burgers with Roasted Red Pepper Spread

Prep Time: 30 minutes | Cook Time: 5 minutes | Serves: 4

1 tablespoon baking powder
1 tablespoon kosher salt
2 teaspoons freshly ground black pepper
2 teaspoons sweet paprika
2 pounds ground lamb
6 garlic cloves, grated
Vegetable oil, for oiling the foil

8 pita rounds
½ cup sour cream
½ cup roasted red pepper spread
1 small red onion, thinly sliced
2 medium tomatoes, sliced
16 butter lettuce leaves

1. In a large bowl, combine the baking powder, salt, pepper, and paprika. Add the lamb and garlic and, using your hands, mix until thoroughly combined. 2. Lightly oil 4 pieces of aluminum foil slightly larger than the size of the pitas. Divide the mixture evenly among them. Form into four ¼-inch-thick patties, leaving a small border around the edges of the foil. 3. To install grill grate, position it flat on top of the heating element so it sits in place, then close hood. Use pellet scoop to pour pellets into smoke box until filled to top. 4. Select GRILL. Select WOODFIRE FLAVOR. Set grill temperature to HI. Set the time to 4 minutes. Select START/STOP to begin preheating. 5. When unit beeps to signify it has preheated and ADD FOOD displays, open hood and slide your palm underneath one of the pieces of foil, and quickly turn the patty over onto the grate. Peel the foil off the top of the patty. Repeat with the remaining pieces. Close hood and grill for 4 minutes, flipping halfway through. Transfer to plates. 6. Put the pita rounds on the grate. Close the hood and grill for 30 to 60 seconds, or just until grill marks appear. Transfer to a work surface. 7. Spread the sour cream on half the pita rounds and the red pepper spread on the remainder. Place one patty on each red pepper spread pita; layer with onion, tomatoes, and lettuce; and top with the sour cream pitas. Quarter each burger and serve immediately.

Garlicky Lamb Chops

Prep Time: 15 minutes | Cook Time: 10 minutes | Serves: 4

2 tablespoons paprika
2 teaspoons salt
2 teaspoons finely chopped fresh rosemary leaves
3 garlic cloves, finely chopped

½ teaspoon black pepper
¼ cup olive oil
8 large (about 4-ounce) lamb loin chops

1. In a small bowl, whisk the paprika, salt, rosemary, garlic, pepper, and olive oil to blend well. Coat both sides of each chop with the marinade and place the chops on a plate. Cover and refrigerate to marinate for 1 to 4 hours. 2. To install grill grate, position it flat on top of the heating element so it sits in place, then close hood. Use pellet scoop to pour pellets into smoke box until filled to top. 3. Select GRILL. Select WOODFIRE FLAVOR. Set grill temperature to HI. Set the time to 10 minutes. Select START/STOP to begin preheating. 4. When unit beeps to signify it has preheated and ADD FOOD displays, open hood and place the chops on the grill grate. Close hood and grill for 10 minutes, flipping halfway through. 5. Let the chops rest for 5 minutes, then serve immediately.

Lemony Rack of Lamb

Prep Time: 15 minutes | Cook Time: 12 minutes | Serves: 2

2 tablespoons paprika
2 teaspoons salt
½ teaspoon garlic powder
½ teaspoon onion powder

½ teaspoon black pepper
1 small (1½-pound) whole rack of lamb, cut into individual chops
Juice of 2 lemons

1. In small bowl, stir together the salt, garlic powder, paprika, onion powder, and pepper until thoroughly combined. Coat each lamb chop with lemon juice, then coat the entire chop with the seasoning mix. 2. Put the seasoned lamb chops in a large bowl, cover, and refrigerate to marinate for 1 to 3 hours. 3. To install grill grate, position it flat on top of the heating element so it sits in place, then close hood. Use pellet scoop to pour pellets into smoke box until filled to top. 4. Select GRILL. Select WOODFIRE FLAVOR. Set grill temperature to HI. Set the time to 12 minutes. Select START/STOP to begin preheating. 5. When unit beeps to signify it has preheated and ADD FOOD displays, open hood and place the chops on the grill grate. Close hood and grill for 12 minutes, flipping halfway through. 6. Let the chops rest for 5 minutes, then serve immediately.

Smoked Venison Steaks with Blackberry Sauce

Prep Time: 20 minutes | Cook Time: 1 hour | Serves: 4

4 (7- to 8-ounce) venison steaks
1½ tablespoons vegetable oil
1¼ teaspoons kosher salt, plus ⅛ teaspoon
1⅛ teaspoons freshly ground black pepper, divided
1 teaspoon ancho chile powder
5 tablespoons unsalted butter, divided

1 medium shallot, minced
2 cups fresh blackberries, plus more for garnish
½ teaspoon balsamic vinegar
1 cup port wine
1 cup vegetable stock
⅛ teaspoon allspice

1. Brush the steaks on both sides with vegetable oil. In a small bowl, combine 1¼ teaspoons of salt, 1 teaspoon of black pepper, and the chile powder and rub the mixture into both sides of the steaks. 2. To install the grill grate, position it flat on top of the heating element so it sits in place. 3. Place the steaks on the grill grate, then close the hood. 4. Use the pellet scoop to pour pellets into the smoke box until filled to the top. Select SMOKER. Set grill temperature to 225°F and time to 1 hour. Select START/STOP to begin cooking. 5. Meanwhile, melt 3 tablespoons of butter in a medium skillet over medium heat, then add the shallot and cook for 2 minutes. Add the blackberries, balsamic vinegar, and port wine, then increase the heat to high and bring the mixture to a boil. Once boiling, reduce the heat to medium-high and simmer until the liquid has reduced by 70 percent. Add the vegetable stock, allspice, remaining ⅛ teaspoon of salt, and remaining ⅛ teaspoon of pepper, and continue simmering until sauce has thickened to a syrup-like consistency. Add the remaining 2 tablespoons of butter and stir through. 6. Strain the sauce through a sieve to remove the blackberry seeds. Return to the pan, cover, and keep warm. 7. Once the venison steaks are done, remove them from the smoker and let rest for 10 minutes. Top with the sauce, garnish with a few fresh blackberries, and serve.

Yummy Lamb Kebabs

Prep Time: 15 minutes | Cook Time: 15 minutes | Serves: 6

1 (2-pound) leg of lamb, cut into 1-inch cubes
½ white onion, cut into 1-inch pieces
1 green bell pepper, cut into 1-inch pieces
1 red bell pepper, cut into 1-inch pieces

½ pound cherry tomatoes
Kosher salt
Freshly ground black pepper

1. If using wooden skewers, soak them in water for 30 to 60 minutes. 2. Prepare the kebabs, making sure to leave 2 to 3 inches at either end: Thread the skewers alternating lamb, onion, lamb, green bell pepper, lamb, red bell pepper, lamb, cherry tomato, lamb, leaving a small gap between each ingredient. 3. Season the kebabs with salt and pepper to taste. 4. To install grill grate, position it flat on top of the heating element so it sits in place, then close hood. Use pellet scoop to pour pellets into smoke box until filled to top. 5. Select GRILL. Select WOODFIRE FLAVOR. Set grill temperature to HI. Set the time to 10 minutes. Select START/STOP to begin preheating. 6. When unit beeps to signify it has preheated and ADD FOOD displays, open hood and place the kebabs on the grill grate. Close hood and grill for 10 minutes, flipping halfway through. 7. Remove the kebabs from the grill and serve immediately.

Lamb-Mushroom Burgers

Prep Time: 10 minutes | Cook Time: 12 minutes | Serves: 6

2 pounds ground lamb, preferably from the shoulder or leg
1 cup finely chopped fresh white mushrooms
1 tablespoon finely minced garlic
2 teaspoons finely minced fresh rosemary
1 tablespoon kosher salt

1 tablespoon coarsely ground black pepper
6 slices fontina cheese
3 tablespoons unsalted butter, at room temperature
6 whole-wheat buns or whole-wheat pita breads
Tzatziki Sauce (optional)

1. In a large bowl, using a light hand, gently work the lamb, mushrooms, garlic, rosemary, salt, and pepper together. Divide the mixture into 6 equal portions and gently form into 1-inch-thick patties. Take your thumb and make a good ¼-inch depression in the middle of each patty; this will keep them from puffing up on the grill. Refrigerate until ready to cook. 2. To install grill grate, position it flat on top of the heating element so it sits in place, then close hood. Use pellet scoop to pour pellets into smoke box until filled to top. 3. Select GRILL. Select WOODFIRE FLAVOR. Set grill temperature to HI. Set the time to 12 minutes. Select START/STOP to begin preheating. 4. When unit beeps to signify it has preheated and ADD FOOD displays, open hood and place the patties on the grill grate. Close hood and grill for 12 minutes, flipping halfway through. When you turn the burgers, place a slice of cheese on top of each. With about 2 minutes left in the cooking time, butter the buns and place them, cut side down, on the grill to toast. 5. When done, transfer the burgers and buns to a warm platter. Place a burger on the bottom half of each bun and top with the tzatziki.

Lemon-Oregano Smoked Leg of Lamb

Prep Time: 25 minutes | Cook Time: 2½ hours | Serves: 8

Zest and juice of 2 lemons
2 tablespoons olive oil
4 garlic cloves, minced
1 medium shallot, minced
¼ cup finely chopped fresh oregano

2 teaspoons finely chopped fresh thyme
2 teaspoons salt
1½ teaspoons freshly ground black pepper
1 (4-pound) boneless leg of lamb

1. In a nonreactive bowl, combine the lemon zest, lemon juice, olive oil, garlic, shallot, oregano, thyme, salt, and black pepper. Set aside. 2. Remove any large clumps of fat and silver skin from the surface of the lamb. Pat the entire leg dry. Unroll the lamb leg to expose the inner portion. Brush with some of the lemon-oregano mixture, then turn it over and brush the rest of the mixture on the outer part. Reroll the lamb and place into a glass baking dish. Cover tightly with plastic wrap and marinate in the refrigerator for 4 hours. 3. When ready to cook, remove the lamb leg from the refrigerator, uncover, and secure the roll with kitchen twine. Let stand at room temperature for 30 minutes. 4. To install the grill grate, position it flat on top of the heating element so it sits in place. 5. Place the lamb on the grill grate, then close the hood. 6. Use the pellet scoop to pour pellets into the smoke box until filled to the top. Select SMOKER. Set grill temperature to 250°F and time to 2½ hours. Select START/STOP to begin cooking. 7. Remove the lamb from the smoker, tent with aluminum foil, and let rest for 10 minutes. Remove the twine, cut the lamb into ½-inch-thick slices, and serve.

Herb-Smoked Rack of Lamb

Prep Time: 25 minutes | Cook Time: 1 hour 30 minutes | Serves: 6

2 (2-pound) racks of lamb
¼ cup unsalted butter, softened
3 tablespoons Dijon mustard
2 tablespoons red wine vinegar
4 garlic cloves, minced
2½ teaspoons kosher salt

2 teaspoons Worcestershire sauce
2 teaspoons finely chopped fresh rosemary
2 teaspoons finely chopped fresh thyme
2 teaspoons finely chopped fresh marjoram
½ teaspoon freshly ground black pepper

1. Remove any large clumps of fat and silver skin from the rack of lamb. 2. In a medium bowl, combine the softened butter, Dijon mustard, red wine vinegar, garlic, salt, Worcestershire sauce, rosemary, thyme, marjoram, and black pepper. Apply this mixture onto the meat of the racks, avoiding the bones. 3. To install the grill grate, position it flat on top of the heating element so it sits in place. 4. Place the racks on the grill grate, bone-side down, then close the hood. 5. Use the pellet scoop to pour pellets into the smoke box until filled to the top. Select SMOKER. Set grill temperature to 225°F and time to 1½ hours. Select START/STOP to begin cooking. 6. Remove from the smoker and let rest for 10 minutes before carving.

Pineapple-Flavored Venison Loin Roast

Prep Time: 20 minutes | Cook Time: 2 hours | Serves: 4

1 (1- to 1½-pound) venison loin roast
½ cup pineapple juice
2 tablespoons dark rum
2½ tablespoons soy sauce
1 tablespoon vegetable oil

1½ teaspoons grated fresh ginger
4 garlic cloves, minced
1 to 2 teaspoons chili sauce (such as sambal oelek or sriracha)
¼ teaspoon white pepper
½ teaspoon salt

1. Place the venison loin in a resealable plastic bag. In a medium bowl, combine the pineapple juice, rum, soy sauce, vegetable oil, ginger, garlic, chili sauce, and white pepper. Pour the marinade over the venison and work it into the meat. Seal the bag and place in the refrigerator for 6 to 12 hours. 2. Remove the loin from the refrigerator and discard the excess marinade. Season the loin with the salt. 3. To install the grill grate, position it flat on top of the heating element so it sits in place. 4. Place the loin on the grill grate, then close the hood. 5. Use the pellet scoop to pour pellets into the smoke box until filled to the top. Select SMOKER. Set grill temperature to 225°F and time to 2 hours. Select START/STOP to begin cooking. 6. Promptly remove the loin from the smoker and let it rest for 10 minutes. Slice and serve.

Smoked Leg of Lamb

Prep Time: 15 minutes | Cook Time: 1 hour | Serves: 10

1 (6- to 8-pound) boneless leg of lamb

2 batches Rosemary-Garlic Lamb Seasoning

1. Using your hands, rub the lamb leg with the seasoning, rubbing it under and around any netting. 2. To install the grill grate, position it flat on top of the heating element so it sits in place. 3. Place the lamb on the grill grate, then close the hood. 4. Use the pellet scoop to pour pellets into the smoke box until filled to the top. Select SMOKER. Set grill temperature to 350°F and time to 1 hour. Select START/STOP to begin cooking. 5. Remove the lamb from the grill and let it rest for 20 to 30 minutes, before removing the netting, slicing, and serving.

Rosemary-Garlic Smoked Rack of Lamb

Prep Time: 25 minutes | Cook Time: 4 hours | Serves: 8

1 (2-pound) rack of lamb

1 batch Rosemary-Garlic Lamb Seasoning

1. Using a boning knife, score the bottom fat portion of the rib meat. 2. Using your hands, rub the rack of lamb all over with the seasoning, making sure it penetrates into the scored fat. 3. To install the grill grate, position it flat on top of the heating element so it sits in place. 4. Place the rack on the grill grate, fat-side up. Then close the hood. 5. Use the pellet scoop to pour pellets into the smoke box until filled to the top. Select SMOKER. Set grill temperature to 225°F and time to 4 hours. Select START/STOP to begin cooking. 6. Remove the rack from the grill and let it rest for 20 to 30 minutes, before slicing it into individual ribs to serve.

Grilled Lamb Steaks

Prep Time: 15 minutes | Cook Time: 12 minutes | Serves: 6

4 to 6 bone-in lamb steaks
Kosher salt

Freshly ground black pepper
1½ cups Western Kentucky Mutton Dip

1. Season both sides of each steak with a few pinches of salt and pepper. 2. To install grill grate, position it flat on top of the heating element so it sits in place. Wipe a little vegetable oil on the grill grates to prevent sticking, then close hood. Use pellet scoop to pour pellets into smoke box until filled to top. 3. Select GRILL. Select WOODFIRE FLAVOR. Set grill temperature to HI. Set the time to 12 minutes. Select START/STOP to begin preheating. 4. When unit beeps to signify it has preheated and ADD FOOD displays, open hood and place the steaks on the grill grate. Close hood and grill for 12 minutes and flip them every 2 to 3 minutes, basting with the mutton dip after every flip. A meat thermometer inserted into the center of the meat should read 130°F. 5. Allow the steaks to rest 10 minutes before serving.

Herbed Ground Lamb Kebabs

Prep Time: 30 minutes | Cook Time: 8 minutes | Serves: 4

2 pounds ground lamb
2 garlic cloves, finely chopped
2 tablespoons finely chopped fresh parsley
1 tablespoon finely chopped fresh dill
1 tablespoon finely chopped fresh mint
1 tablespoon finely chopped fresh cilantro

1 teaspoon ground coriander
1 teaspoon ground cumin
1 teaspoon paprika
1 teaspoon salt
½ teaspoon black pepper
½ teaspoon ground cinnamon

1. In a large bowl, combine the lamb, garlic, parsley, dill, mint, cilantro, coriander, cumin, paprika, salt, pepper, and cinnamon. Using clean hands, mix until just combined. Do not overmix. 2. Evenly divide the mixture into 8 portions on a cutting board and press each into a rectangle about 4 inches long and 2 inches thick. Lay a metal skewer lengthwise in the center of the rectangles and use your hands to wrap the meat around the skewers, forming a cylinder. Refrigerate for 30 minutes. 3. To install grill grate, position it flat on top of the heating element so it sits in place. Lightly oil the grill grate and close hood. Use pellet scoop to pour pellets into smoke box until filled to top. 4. Select GRILL. Select WOODFIRE FLAVOR. Set grill temperature to HI. Set the time to 8 minutes. Select START/STOP to begin preheating. 5. When unit beeps to signify it has preheated and ADD FOOD displays, open hood and place the lamb kebabs on the grill grate. Close hood and grill for 8 minutes, turning every 2 to 3 minutes, until the internal temperature reaches 160°F. 6. Let the meat rest for 5 minutes, then serve as desired.

Chapter 7 Pork Recipes

Honey Mustard Smoked Pulled Pork

Prep Time: 10 minutes | Cook Time: 12 hours | Serves: 4

1 (6- to 8-pound) bone-in pork shoulder
2 tablespoons honey mustard

Sweet Brown Sugar Rub

1. Rub the pork shoulder with the mustard and season with a generous amount of the rub, massaging it into the meat. 2. To install the grill grate, position it flat on top of the heating element so it sits in place. 3. Place the pork shoulder on the grill grate, then close the hood. 4. Use the pellet scoop to pour pellets into the smoke box until filled to the top. Select SMOKER. Set grill temperature to 250°F and time to 12 hours. Select START/STOP to begin cooking. 5. Remove the shoulder from the grill and let rest for 1 hour or more, until you're able to pull the pork with your hands without burning yourself. 6. Pull out the bone and pull the pork apart, using just your fingers.

Pork Rollups

Prep Time: 30 minutes | Cook Time: 1½ hours | Serves: 10

1-pound ground pork
1-pound bratwurst sausage, casings removed
1 tablespoon brown sugar
1 teaspoon paprika
½ teaspoon chili powder

½ teaspoon onion powder
¼ teaspoon cayenne pepper
1-pound bacon
1 cup store-bought barbecue sauce

1. Combine the ground pork, bratwurst sausage, brown sugar, paprika, chili powder, onion powder, and cayenne in a large bowl. Form the mixture into small rectangles about 1-inch thick and 2 inches long. 2. Cut the bacon strips in half lengthwise and separate them. Set a rectangle on one end of each strip of bacon and roll it up. Secure each rollup with a toothpick. 3. To install the grill grate, position it flat on top of the heating element so it sits in place. 4. Place the rollups on the grill grate, then close the hood. 5. Use the pellet scoop to pour pellets into the smoke box until filled to the top. Select SMOKER. Set grill temperature to 250°F and time to 1 hour. Select START/STOP to begin cooking. Flip them and cook for another 30 minutes. 6. During the last 30 minutes of cook time, brush the rollups with barbecue sauce twice. Coat one side, then 15 minutes later, turn them over and brush with sauce on the other side. They are done once they reach an internal temperature of 175°F.

Beer-Glazed Ham

Prep Time: 20 minutes | Cook Time: 4 hours | Serves: 10

1 (6- to 7-pound) ham, unsliced and bone-in
2 tablespoons whole cloves, for studding
2½ cups root beer
1 cup packed dark brown sugar

2 tablespoons melted butter
1½ tablespoons Dijon mustard
1 tablespoon red wine vinegar
2 teaspoons grated fresh ginger

1. Set the ham on a large cutting board. Blot it dry with paper towels and stud the top surface with cloves, spacing them an inch apart in a diamond pattern. 2. To install the grill grate, position it flat on top of the heating element so it sits in place. 3. Place the ham on the grill grate, then close the hood. 4. Use the pellet scoop to pour pellets into the smoke box until filled to the top. Select SMOKER. Set grill temperature to 225°F and time to 2 hours. Select START/STOP to begin cooking. 5. In a medium bowl, combine the root beer, brown sugar, butter, Dijon mustard, red wine vinegar, and ginger. Cover and set aside until ready to use. 6. After 2 hours of cooking, brush the ham with the glaze. Repeat glazing every 30 to 40 minutes until the ham reaches an internal temperature of 140°F, about 2 hours. 7. Carefully remove the ham from the smoker and place it on a clean cutting board. Let it rest for 15 to 30 minutes, then carve and serve.

Texas Pork Steaks

Prep Time: 20 minutes | Cook Time: 2½ hours | Serves: 4

½ cup brown sugar
2 tablespoons kosher salt
1 tablespoon chili powder
2 teaspoons freshly ground black pepper

1 teaspoon onion powder
4 (1-inch-thick) pork steaks
½ cup apple juice

1. In a small bowl, combine the brown sugar, salt, chili powder, pepper, and onion powder. Apply the rub liberally to both sides and edges of the pork steaks. 2. To install the grill grate, position it flat on top of the heating element so it sits in place. 3. Place the pork steaks on the grill grate, then close the hood. 4. Use the pellet scoop to pour pellets into the smoke box until filled to the top. Select SMOKER. Set grill temperature to 250°F and time to 1 hour. Select START/STOP to begin cooking. 5. Pour the apple juice into a spray bottle. After 1 hour of cooking, spritz the steaks with the apple juice. Continue to cook, spritzing every 30 minutes, until they reach an internal temperature of between 180°F and 185°F, about 1½ to 2 hours. 6. Remove the steaks, let them rest for 10 to 15 minutes, and serve.

Smoked Sweet Ham

Prep Time: 10 minutes | Cook Time: 4 hours | Serves: 6

41 (8- to 10-pound) precooked ham
Sweet Brown Sugar Rub

3 tablespoons maple syrup

1. Generously season the ham with the rub, massaging the rub all over the ham. 2. Place the ham in a baking pan. 3. To install the grill grate, position it flat on top of the heating element so it sits in place. 4. Place the pan on the grill grate, then close the hood. 5. Use the pellet scoop to pour pellets into the smoke box until filled to the top. Select SMOKER. Set grill temperature to 180°F and time to 4 hours. Select START/STOP to begin cooking. 6. After 1 hour during cooking, drizzle the ham with the maple syrup. 7. Remove the ham from the grill and let rest for 5 to 10 minutes. 8. Thinly slice the ham and serve.

Smoked Spicy Pork Tenderloins

Prep Time: 5 minutes | Cook Time: 2 hours | Serves: 4

2 (1-pound) pork tenderloins

Spicy Rub

1. Generously season the tenderloins with the rub, massaging it into the meat. 2. To install the grill grate, position it flat on top of the heating element so it sits in place. 3. Place the tenderloins on the grill grate, then close the hood. 4. Use the pellet scoop to pour pellets into the smoke box until filled to the top. Select SMOKER. Set grill temperature to 225°F and time to 2 hours. Select START/STOP to begin cooking. 5. Remove the tenderloins from the grill and let rest for 10 minutes. 6. Slice the tenderloins and serve.

Lemony Pork Kebabs

Prep Time: 25 minutes | Cook Time: 1½ hours | Serves: 5

1 cup ketchup
½ cup soy sauce
½ cup lemon-lime soda
Juice of 1 lemon
2 garlic cloves, minced
2 tablespoons olive oil

1 tablespoon sriracha
1 tablespoon white sugar
1 teaspoon onion powder
½ teaspoon salt
½ teaspoon freshly ground black pepper
1 (3-pound) pork butt or pork tenderloin

1. In a large nonreactive bowl, combine the ketchup, soy sauce, soda, lemon juice, garlic, olive oil, sriracha, sugar, onion powder, salt, and black pepper. Reserve ¾ cup of the marinade for basting. 2. Trim away excess fat from the pork and cut it into 1¼-inch cubes. Place the pork into the bowl with the marinade and toss to coat. Cover the bowl tightly with plastic wrap, and refrigerate for 6 to 10 hours. If using wooden skewers, soak them in tepid water 30 minutes before using. 3. Remove the pork from the refrigerator and discard the excess marinade. Thread the pork onto skewers, about 5 pieces per skewer. 4. To install the grill grate, position it flat on top of the heating element so it sits in place. 5. Place the skewers on the grill grate, then close the hood. 6. Use the pellet scoop to pour pellets into the smoke box until filled to the top. Select SMOKER. Set grill temperature to 250°F and time to 1½ hours. Select START/STOP to begin cooking, turning the kebabs after 1 hour. During the last 30 minutes of cook time, baste the skewers with the reserved marinade. 6. Once the internal temperature of the kebabs reaches 155°F, remove from the smoker and let them rest for 10 minutes before serving.

Yummy Barbecue-Spiced Pork Tenderloin

Prep Time: 15 minutes | Cook Time: 24 minutes | Serves: 4

¼ cup paprika
2 tablespoons light brown sugar
1 tablespoon salt
1 tablespoon black pepper

1 tablespoon chili powder
1 tablespoon garlic powder
1 tablespoon onion powder
1 (2- to 3-pound) pork tenderloin roast

1. In a small bowl, stir together the paprika, brown sugar, salt, pepper, chili powder, garlic powder, and onion powder until blended. Coat all sides of the pork tenderloin with the rub. Cover and let sit at room temperature for 30 minutes. 2. To install grill grate, position it flat on top of the heating element so it sits in place, then close hood. Use pellet scoop to pour pellets into smoke box until filled to top. 3. Select GRILL. Select WOODFIRE FLAVOR. Set grill temperature to LO. Set the time to 24 minutes. Select START/STOP to begin preheating. 4. When unit beeps to signify it has preheated and ADD FOOD displays, open hood and place the pork tenderloin on the grill grate. Close hood and grill for 24 minutes, flipping halfway through. 5. Remove the pork from the grill and let rest for 5 minutes. Cut into ½-inch-thick slices. Serve immediately.

Flavorful BBQ Baby Back Ribs

Prep Time: 30 minutes | Cook Time: 4 hours | Serves: 6

For the Spice Rub:
3 tablespoons cumin seeds, whole
3 tablespoons coriander seeds, whole
3 tablespoons fennel seeds, whole
1 tablespoon allspice berries, whole

3 tablespoons paprika
3 tablespoons chili powder
1 tablespoon garlic powder
1 tablespoon onion powder

For the Baby Back Ribs:
8 pounds baby back pork ribs, trimmed and membranes removed
Flaked sea salt
Freshly ground black pepper
2 cups packed dark brown sugar

2 cups dark molasses
2 cups wildflower honey
2 cups apple cider
½ cup bourbon (or brandy)

To make the spice rub: 1. Preheat a heavy-bottom pan over medium heat on the stovetop. 2. Combine the cumin, coriander, fennel, and allspice. Toast the spices for about 5 minutes, until they're fragrant and smoky, gently tossing them to toast evenly. Let cool slightly. Grind the spices in a mortar with a pestle or in a clean spice or coffee grinder until smooth. Transfer to a small bowl. 3. Stir in the paprika, chili powder, garlic powder, and onion powder. Store in an airtight container.

To make the baby back ribs: 1. Rub the spice mixture evenly over both sides of the ribs. Season them with salt and pepper. 2. To install the grill grate, position it flat on top of the heating element so it sits in place. 3. Place the ribs on the grill grate, flesh-side up, leaving space between them. Close the hood. 4. Use the pellet scoop to pour pellets into the smoke box until filled to the top. Select SMOKER. Set grill temperature to 250°F and time to 2 hours. Select START/STOP to begin cooking. 5. On a large sheet of aluminum foil, prepare a bed of brown sugar drizzled with the molasses and honey. 6. Place the ribs, flesh-side down, onto the sugar bed. Add the apple cider and bourbon. Tightly wrap the ribs in the foil and return them to the smoker. Smoke for about 2 hours more. Remove the ribs from the smoker and let rest for 20 minutes. 7. Unwrap the foil, remove the ribs, and serve with the sauce that developed in the foil.

Rosemary Smoked Pork Chops with Pears

Prep Time: 20 minutes | Cook Time: 1 hour 30 minutes | Serves: 4

1 tablespoon extra-virgin olive oil, plus more for brushing
1 tablespoon unsalted butter, melted
4 bone-in pork chops
2 tablespoons flaked sea salt
Freshly ground black pepper

¼ cup smoked paprika
8 rosemary sprigs
2 Bosc or Bartlett pears, halved and cored
2 limes, halved

1. Pour the olive oil and the melted butter in a baking pan. 2. Brush the pork chops all over with olive oil. Season with salt, pepper, and paprika. Press 2 rosemary sprigs into the oiled surface of each chop. 3. Place the chops, rosemary-side down, in the baking pan. 4. To install the grill grate, position it flat on top of the heating element so it sits in place. 5. Place the pan on the grill grate, then close the hood. 6. Use the pellet scoop to pour pellets into the smoke box until filled to the top. Select SMOKER. Set grill temperature to 275°F and time to 1½ hours. Select START/STOP to begin cooking. 7. Place the pears in the skillet, flesh-side down. Cook for about 20 minutes, until tender. Remove and set aside. 8. Transfer the pork to a cutting board. Loosely tent it with aluminum foil and let it rest for 10 minutes. 9. Serve the chops topped with any of the liquid that accumulated while resting, a thinly sliced pear, and half a lime for squeezing.

Cheese Ham Sandwiches

Prep Time: 20 minutes | Cook Time: 3 minutes | Serves: 4

4 french rolls
¼ cup yellow mustard
8 slices deli ham
2 cups shredded or chopped cuban roast pork (pernil)

40 dill pickle chips
4 Swiss cheese slices
4 tablespoons (½ stick) unsalted butter, softened

1. Spread the mustard on the cut sides of each roll. 2. Layer the ham, pork, pickles, and cheese on the bottom half of the rolls, in that order. Finish with the top half of the rolls and spread the butter on top. 3. To install the grill grate, position it flat on top of the heating element so it sits in place. 4. Select the BAKE function. Adjust the temperature to 400°F and time to 3 minutes. Select START/STOP to begin preheating. 5. When preheating is complete, open the hood and place the sandwiches on the grate. Once the hood is closed, cooking will begin and the timer will start counting down. 6. When cook time reaches zero, the grill will beep and DONE will appear on the display. Remove food from grill grate. Serve immediately.

Homemade Dirty Rice

Prep Time: 15 minutes | Cook Time: 30 minutes | Serves: 8

1 pound smoked sausage, such as andouille, removed from the casing and crumbled
8 ounces chicken livers, trimmed of membranes
2 tablespoons unsalted butter
2 cups finely diced red onion
1 cup finely diced celery
1 cup finely diced green bell pepper
6 garlic cloves, chopped

3 cups cooked white rice
1¼ cups low-sodium chicken broth
1 tablespoon kosher salt
1 tablespoon sweet paprika
2 teaspoons cayenne pepper
1 teaspoon freshly ground black pepper
1 teaspoon dried oregano
½ teaspoon ground cinnamon

1. To install the grill grate, position it flat on top of the heating element so it sits in place. 2. Select the BAKE function. Adjust the temperature to 500°F and time to 8 minutes. Select START/STOP to begin preheating. 3. Put the sausage and chicken livers in a baking pan. 4. When preheating is complete, open the hood and place the pan on the grate. Once the hood is closed, cooking will begin and the timer will start counting down, stirring once. Using a slotted spoon, transfer to a cutting board. Once cool enough to handle, finely chop. 5. Add the butter, onion, celery, bell pepper, and garlic to the baking pan. Close the hood and cook, stirring occasionally, for 6 to 7 minutes or until slightly softened. Remove from the heat. 6. Reduce the grill temperature to 400°F. 7. Put the baking pan back on the grate. Add the cooked rice, broth, sausage and chicken liver mixture, salt, paprika, cayenne, pepper, oregano, and cinnamon to the pan and stir to combine. Close the hood and bring to a simmer. Cook for 4 to 6 minutes or until the liquid and seasonings are absorbed. Serve immediately.

Chinese Teriyaki Pork Ribs

Prep Time: 15 minutes | Cook Time: 2½ hours | Serves: 6

½ cup teriyaki sauce
¼ cup soy sauce
¼ cup ketchup
2 tablespoons hoisin sauce

4 garlic cloves, finely chopped
1 teaspoon Chinese five-spice powder
4 or 5 drops red food coloring
1 full (3- to 4-pound) rack pork baby back ribs

1. In medium bowl, whisk the teriyaki sauce, soy sauce, ketchup, hoisin sauce, garlic, five-spice powder, and food coloring until blended. Place the ribs in a large shallow baking dish and pour two-thirds of the marinade over the ribs. Turn the ribs over to coat the other side. Cover the dish and refrigerate to marinate for 2 hours to overnight, turning every 30 minutes. Refrigerate the remaining marinade. 2. Remove the ribs from the refrigerator about 20 minutes before cooking to let the pork come close to room temperature. 3. To install the grill grate, position it flat on top of the heating element so it sits in place. 4. Place the ribs on the grill grate, then close the hood. 5. Use the pellet scoop to pour pellets into the smoke box until filled to the top. Select SMOKER. Set grill temperature to 325°F and time to 2½ hours. Select START/STOP to begin cooking, turning 3 or 4 times during cooking. 6. At the 2-hour mark, begin basting the ribs with the reserved marinade from the refrigerator every 10 minutes until fully cooked. The ribs are fully cooked when they feel tender when probed with a metal skewer or meat thermometer and/or the rack begins to bend easily when picked up at one end with tongs. 7. Let the ribs rest 10 minutes. Cut the ribs into individual portions and serve immediately.

Smoked Spare Ribs with Spiced Apple Glaze

Prep Time: 1 hour | Cook Time: 5 hours | Serves: 6

2 slabs of St. Louis–cut pork spare ribs
1 cup Spicy Rum Wet Rub
1 cup apple cider

¼ cup apple cider vinegar
1 cup Sticky Spiced Apple Glaze

1. Remove the membrane from the back of the ribs: Use a butter knife to loosen the tough silver skin at one end. Grip the loosened membrane with a paper towel and pull firmly. 2. Coat the front and back of the ribs liberally with the Spicy Rum Wet Rub. 3. Wrap the rubbed ribs in plastic wrap and refrigerate for 1 hour. 4. To install the grill grate, position it flat on top of the heating element so it sits in place. 5. Place the ribs on the grill grate, bone-side down, then close the hood. 6. Use the pellet scoop to pour pellets into the smoke box until filled to the top. Select SMOKER. Set grill temperature to 250°F and time to 3 hours. Select START/STOP to begin cooking. 7. In a medium bowl, mix together the apple cider and vinegar. 8. After 3 hours, remove the ribs from the smoker and place onto separate sheets of heavy-duty aluminum foil. Spritz the ribs with the apple cider mixture and wrap them tightly, being careful not to tear the foil. 9. Place the ribs back on the smoker and cook for an additional 2 hours. 10. Remove the ribs from the smoker and transfer them to an aluminum tray. 11. Unwrap the ribs and baste them with the Spiced Apple Glaze. 12. Place the ribs back onto the cooker until the glaze caramelizes and the ribs tighten up a bit. 13. A toothpick or meat probe poked in the meat between the bones should pass through with very little resistance, like warm butter. 14. Remove the ribs from the heat and let rest for 10 to 15 minutes before slicing.

Sweet Barbecue Riblets

Prep Time: 15 minutes | Cook Time: 2 hours | Serves: 5

For the Riblets:
2½ pounds pork riblets
¼ cup Dijon mustard (use more if needed)

2 tablespoons plus 2 teaspoons All-Purpose Rub

For the Sauce:
½ cup ketchup
½ cup apple jelly
¼ cup water
¼ cup apple cider vinegar
¼ cup dark brown sugar

1 teaspoon All-Purpose Rub
1 tablespoon blackstrap molasses
½ teaspoon Worcestershire sauce
1 tablespoon butter

To make the riblets: 1. Coat each riblet section with Dijon mustard. Then season the riblets on both sides with the All-Purpose Rub. 2. To install the grill grate, position it flat on top of the heating element so it sits in place. 3. Place the riblets on the grill grate, then close the hood. 4. Use the pellet scoop to pour pellets into the smoke box until filled to the top. Select SMOKER. Set grill temperature to 250°F and time to 1 hour. Select START/STOP to begin cooking.

To make the sauce: 1. Meanwhile, in a small saucepan over medium-high heat, combine the ketchup, apple jelly, water, apple cider vinegar, brown sugar, and All-Purpose Rub and simmer for 1 minute. Reduce the heat to medium-low, and simmer for 5 minutes, stirring occasionally. Add the molasses and Worcestershire sauce, and simmer for 2 more minutes. Reduce the heat to low, if needed. Add the butter and stir until melted. Remove from heat, cover, and set aside. 2. After 1 hour of cooking, baste the riblets with the sauce every 15 minutes during the remaining hour of cook time. 3. Once the riblets reach an internal temperature of 195°F, they are done. Remove from the smoker, let them rest for about 10 minutes, and serve as is, or slice into individual riblets.

Garlic-Honey Pork Chops

Prep Time: 15 minutes | Cook Time: 17 minutes | Serves: 4

4 (10- to 12-ounce) bone-in pork loin or rib chops
1 tablespoon salt, divided
1 teaspoon black pepper or crushed rainbow peppercorns, divided
4 tablespoons (½ stick) butter
6 garlic cloves, minced

⅓ cup chicken broth
⅓ cup honey
1 tablespoon chopped fresh rosemary or sage leaves
1 teaspoon apple cider vinegar
2 scallions, both white and green parts, thinly sliced

1. Season the pork chops with 1½ teaspoons of salt and ½ teaspoon of pepper. Cover and let sit at room temperature while you make the sauce. 2. In a small saucepan over medium-low heat, melt the butter. Add the garlic and sauté for about 30 seconds, just until fragrant. Whisk in the chicken broth, honey, rosemary, and vinegar. Season with the remaining 1½ teaspoons of salt and ½ teaspoon of pepper. Increase the heat to medium-high and cook the sauce for about 5 minutes, stirring, until it reduces and thickens slightly. Let cool. 3. To install grill grate, position it flat on top of the heating element so it sits in place. Oil the grill grate and close hood. Use pellet scoop to pour pellets into smoke box until filled to top. 4. Select GRILL. Select WOODFIRE FLAVOR. Set grill temperature to HI. Set the time to 12 minutes. Select START/STOP to begin preheating. 5. When unit beeps to signify it has preheated and ADD FOOD displays, open hood and place the pork chops on the grill grate. Close hood and grill for 12 minutes, flipping halfway through. Baste the chops with the sauce frequently while cooking. Reserve the remaining sauce. 6. Let the chops rest for 5 minutes. Arrange the pork chops on a serving platter and drizzle the remaining sauce over the chops. Sprinkle with scallions before serving.

Grilled Sausages with Onions and Peppers

Prep Time: 15 minutes | Cook Time: 8 minutes | Serves: 4

1 onion, chopped into 1-inch squares
1 green bell pepper, chopped into 1-inch squares
1 red bell pepper, chopped into 1-inch squares
½ teaspoon salt
½ teaspoon black pepper

½ teaspoon red pepper flakes
2 tablespoons olive oil
4 mild or hot Italian sausage links
4 hoagie rolls, split

1. In a large bowl, combine the onion, green and red bell peppers, salt, black pepper, and red pepper flakes. Add the olive oil and toss well until combined and coated. 2. To install grill grate, position it flat on top of the heating element so it sits in place, then close hood. Use pellet scoop to pour pellets into smoke box until filled to top. 3. Select GRILL. Select WOODFIRE FLAVOR. Set grill temperature to HI. Set the time to 8 minutes. Select START/STOP to begin preheating. 4. When unit beeps to signify it has preheated and ADD FOOD displays, open hood and place the sausages on one side of the grill grate. Put the vegetables into a grill pan and place on the grate beside the sausages. Close hood and grill for 8 minutes, turning them every 2 to 3 minutes. 5. Let the sausages rest for 5 minutes, then serve with the grilled onions and peppers in the rolls, or as desired.

Smoked Pork Ham Shanks

Prep Time: 15 minutes | Cook Time: 2½ hours | Serves: 4

4 cups water
¾ cup salt
¾ cup dark brown sugar

2 teaspoons pink curing salt
5 pounds pork shanks

1. In a large resealable plastic container, combine the water, salt, brown sugar, and curing salt. Stir and let it stand until the sugar and salt have dissolved, then stir again. 2. Submerge the pork shanks into the liquid, seal the container, and refrigerate for 1 week. 3. Remove the shanks from the liquid and rinse them under cold water. Place a wire rack on top of a baking sheet. Lightly blot the pork shanks dry, then place them on the wire rack. Refrigerate, uncovered, for 18 to 24 hours. 4. To install the grill grate, position it flat on top of the heating element so it sits in place. 5. Place the ham shanks on the grill grate, then close the hood. 6. Use the pellet scoop to pour pellets into the smoke box until filled to the top. Select SMOKER. Set grill temperature to 200°F and time to 2½ hours. Select START/STOP to begin cooking. 7. Once the shanks have reached an internal temperature of 150°F, remove them from the smoker and let cool for 1 hour before using.

Country-Style Barbecue Pork Ribs

Prep Time: 15 minutes | Cook Time: 20 minutes | Serves: 4

3 pounds boneless country-style pork ribs
1 teaspoon salt

1 teaspoon black pepper
½ cup Kansas City–Style Barbecue Sauce

1. Lightly season the ribs with salt and pepper, coating all sides. 2. To install grill grate, position it flat on top of the heating element so it sits in place. Lightly oil the grill grate and close hood. Use pellet scoop to pour pellets into smoke box until filled to top. 3. Select GRILL. Select WOODFIRE FLAVOR. Set grill temperature to HI. Set the time to 15 minutes. Select START/STOP to begin preheating. 4. When unit beeps to signify it has preheated and ADD FOOD displays, open hood and place the ribs on the grill grate. Close hood and grill for 15 minutes, flipping halfway through. 5. then baste the pork with the sauce and cook for about 5 minutes more, turning often, until they reach an internal temperature of 145°F. 6. Let the pork rest for 5 minutes. Serve with any remaining sauce.

Smoked Bratwursts & Sauerkraut

Prep Time: 15 minutes | Cook Time: 1 hour | Serves: 12

12 bratwurst sausages
3½ to 4 cups sauerkraut
4 cups vegetable broth

2 cups beer of choice
2 garlic cloves
12 hot dog buns

1. To install the grill grate, position it flat on top of the heating element so it sits in place. 2. Place the bratwursts on the grill grate, then close the hood. 3. Use the pellet scoop to pour pellets into the smoke box until filled to the top. Select SMOKER. Set grill temperature to 225°F and time to 1 hour. Select START/STOP to begin cooking. 4. Once the bratwursts have been on the smoker for 20 minutes, place the sauerkraut in an aluminum pan, and place the pan in the smoker for 30 minutes. Remove and let stand for 15 minutes before using. (If making the sauerkraut ahead of time, cool completely after cooking, cover the pan with foil, and store in the refrigerator.) 5. Meanwhile, in a large pot over medium-low heat, combine the vegetable broth, beer, and garlic and cook for 15 minutes. After 15 minutes, reduce to very low heat, or transfer broth mixture to a slow cooker and set temperature on warm. 6. Once the bratwursts have reached an internal temperature of between 160°F and 165°F, place them in the broth mixture until it is time to serve. 7. To serve, place a bratwurst into a hot dog bun and top with sauerkraut.

Easy Smoked Bacon

Prep Time: 5 minutes | Cook Time: 20 minutes | Serves: 6

1 pound thick-sliced pork bacon

1. To install the grill grate, position it flat on top of the heating element so it sits in place. 2. Place the bacon slices on the grill grate, then close the hood. 3. Use the pellet scoop to pour pellets into the smoke box until filled to the top. Select SMOKER. Set grill temperature to 325°F and time to 20 minutes. Select START/STOP to begin cooking. 4. Serve immediately.

Carolina Pulled Pork with Barbecue Sauce

Prep Time: 15 minutes | Cook Time: 8 hours | Serves: 8

For the Pulled Pork:
1 (6- to 8-pound) pork butt
¼ cup brown sugar
1½ tablespoons kosher salt
1 tablespoon dry mustard
1 teaspoon dark chili powder
For the Barbecue Sauce:
1½ cups apple cider vinegar
¼ cup white vinegar
2 tablespoons ketchup
1½ tablespoons brown sugar

2 teaspoons freshly ground black pepper
1 teaspoon onion powder
1 teaspoon granulated garlic
½ cup apple juice, room temperature
2 tablespoons butter

1 tablespoon hot sauce (such as Tabasco)
1 teaspoon red pepper flakes
1 teaspoon salt
1 teaspoon freshly ground black pepper

To make the pulled pork: Trim down the thick layer of fat on the pork butt to about ¼ inch. 2. In a small bowl, combine the brown sugar, salt, dry mustard, chili powder, pepper, onion powder, and granulated garlic. Apply the rub to the entire surface area of the pork butt. Let stand at room temperature for at least 30 minutes. 3. To install the grill grate, position it flat on top of the heating element so it sits in place. 4. Place the seasoned pork butt on the grill grate, then close the hood. 5. Use the pellet scoop to pour pellets into the smoke box until filled to the top. Select SMOKER. Set grill temperature to 225°F and time to 5 hours. Select START/STOP to begin cooking. 6. Once it reaches 160°F, remove the pork and place in a large aluminum pan. Pour the apple juice around the edges of the roast, top with the butter, and seal tightly with aluminum foil. Place the pan back into the smoker for 3 to 4 hours, or until the pork reaches an internal temperature of between 195°F and 205°F. Remove the pan from the smoker but leave it covered. Place the pan into a clean, room-temperature cooler for 1 to 2 hours. If you do not have a cooler, wrap the pan with extra foil, cover tightly with 2 or 3 thick kitchen towels, and store in an unheated oven.

To make the barbecue sauce: 1. Whisk together all ingredients for the barbecue sauce in a medium bowl and let it sit for 10 minutes until the sugar and salt have dissolved. Cover and set aside. 2. Wearing heat-resistant gloves, peel back the foil and break apart the meat inside the pan with the liquid. Lightly coat with the sauce and serve.

Barbecue Baby Back Ribs

Prep Time: 15 minutes | Cook Time: 3 hours 10 minutes | Serves: 4

4 (2- to 2½-pound) racks baby back ribs
3 tablespoons kosher salt

3 tablespoons freshly ground black pepper
⅔ cup kansas city–style barbecue sauce

1. Trim any hanging fat off the ribs. Season with the salt and pepper on both sides. Let rest at room temperature for 1 hour. 2. To install the grill grate, position it flat on top of the heating element so it sits in place. 3. Place the ribs meat-side up on the grill grate, then close the hood. 4. Use the pellet scoop to pour pellets into the smoke box until filled to the top. Select SMOKER. Set grill temperature to 250°F and time to 3 hours. Select START/STOP to begin cooking, flipping halfway through. 5. Baste the ribs with the sauce, close the hood, and cook meat-side up for 10 more minutes or until the sauce is set. Serve immediately.

Cheese Pulled Pork Nachos

Prep Time: 10 minutes | Cook Time: 8 minutes | Serves: 4

3 cups carolina pulled pork
⅓ cup kansas city–style barbecue sauce
4 cups tortilla chips
1 cup shredded monterey jack cheese

1 jalapeño pepper, stemmed and thinly sliced
⅓ cup diced white onion
1 (15-ounce) can black beans, drained and rinsed

1. To install the grill grate, position it flat on top of the heating element so it sits in place. 2. Select the ROAST function. Adjust the temperature to 350°F and time to 8 minutes. Select START/STOP to begin preheating. 3. In a medium bowl, toss the pork with the sauce until thoroughly coated. 4. In a baking pan, layer the tortilla chips, pork, cheese, jalapeño pepper, onion, and beans. 5. When preheating is complete, open the hood and place the pan on the grill grate. Once the hood is closed, cooking will begin and the timer will begin counting down. Cook just until the cheese melts. Serve immediately.

Homemade Pork Belly Burnt Ends

Prep Time: 15 minutes | Cook Time: 5 hours | Serves: 10

1 (4-pound) slab pork belly, 1 to 1¼ inches thick, skin removed
4 tablespoons light brown sugar, divided
1 tablespoon kosher salt
½ tablespoon freshly ground black pepper
1½ teaspoons onion powder
1 teaspoon sweet paprika
½ teaspoon garlic powder
½ teaspoon chili powder
¼ teaspoon ground ginger
¼ teaspoon red pepper flakes
1 cup apple juice
½ cup Blood Orange BBQ Sauce, or store-bought
2 tablespoons cold butter, cut into small chunks

1. In a small bowl, combine 2 tablespoons of brown sugar, salt, pepper, onion powder, paprika, garlic powder, chili powder, ginger, and red pepper flakes. Apply the rub evenly over the entire pork belly. 2. To install the grill grate, position it flat on top of the heating element so it sits in place. 3. Place the pork on the grill grate, then close the hood. 4. Use the pellet scoop to pour pellets into the smoke box until filled to the top. Select SMOKER. Set grill temperature to 250°F and time to 4 hours. Select START/STOP to begin cooking. 5. Pour the apple juice into a spray bottle. After the pork has cooked for 1 hour, spritz it lightly with the apple juice. The surface should be slightly moist. Repeat spritzing as needed. 6. After about 4 hours of cooking, or when the pork belly reaches an internal temperature of 165°F, remove it from the smoker, wrap it in aluminum foil, and return it to the smoker. Cook until the internal temperature reaches 190°F, about 30 minutes. 7. Remove the pork belly, cut into 1-inch cubes, and arrange in a large aluminum pan in an even layer. Top with the Blood Orange BBQ sauce, the remaining 2 tablespoons of brown sugar, and the cold butter pieces. 8. Place the pan back into the smoker for 30 minutes, or until the sauce has caramelized. Remove and let stand for 15 minutes before serving.

Carolina Pulled Pork Potato Hash

Prep Time: 15 minutes | Cook Time: 2 hours | Serves: 8

3 bacon slices
2 large yellow or white onions, diced
4 cups carolina pulled pork
1 pound Yukon gold potatoes, diced
4 cups water
¼ cup apple cider vinegar
1 tablespoon red pepper flakes
1 tablespoon kosher salt
1 tablespoon freshly ground black pepper
2 teaspoons dry mustard
4 tablespoons (½ stick) unsalted butter, melted

1. To install grill grate, position it flat on top of the heating element so it sits in place, then close hood. Use pellet scoop to pour pellets into smoke box until filled to top. 2. Select GRILL. Select WOODFIRE FLAVOR. Set grill temperature to HI. Set the time to 2 minutes. Select START/STOP to begin preheating. 3. When unit beeps to signify it has preheated and ADD FOOD displays, open hood. Put the bacon in a baking pan and place the pan on the grill grate. Close hood and grill for 2 minutes or until browned and crispy around the edges. Transfer to a plate. Once cool enough to handle, crumble. 4. Add the onions to the baking pan, stirring to coat with the bacon fat. Close the hood and cook for 8 to 10 minutes or until softened and browned. 5. Reduce the grill temperature to LO. Add the bacon, pork, potatoes, water, vinegar, red pepper flakes, salt, pepper, and dry mustard; stir to combine. Close the hood and bring to a simmer. Cook for 1 hour 30 minutes, breaking up the potatoes as they soften, or until all the liquid has been absorbed; stir frequently toward the end. Stir in the butter and serve immediately.

Vietnamese Lemongrass Pork Chops

Prep Time: 5 minutes | Cook Time: 5 minutes | Serves: 4

1 (3-inch) piece lemongrass, tough portions discarded, finely chopped
3 tablespoons water
2 tablespoons fish sauce
1 tablespoon light brown sugar
4 (4-ounce) boneless center-cut pork chops

1. In a small saucepan on the stove top, combine the lemongrass, water, fish sauce, and sugar. Heat, stirring, just until it comes to a simmer and the sugar dissolves. Transfer to a shallow heatproof dish. 2. Place the pork between two pieces of plastic wrap; pound to ½-inch thickness. Transfer to the dish with the marinade and turn to coat thoroughly. 3. Marinate at room temperature for 1 hour, turning halfway through. 4. To install grill grate, position it flat on top of the heating element so it sits in place, then close hood. Use pellet scoop to pour pellets into smoke box until filled to top. 5. Select GRILL. Select WOODFIRE FLAVOR. Set grill temperature to HI. Set the time to 5 minutes. Select START/STOP to begin preheating. 6. When unit beeps to signify it has preheated and ADD FOOD displays, open hood. Shake off any excess marinade. Put the pork on the grill grate. Close hood and grill for 5 minutes, flipping halfway through. 7. Serve immediately.

Chapter 8 Snacks and Appetizers

Creamy Smoked Onion Dip

Prep Time: 15 minutes | Cook Time: 1 hour | Serves: 8

2 medium yellow onions, halved vertically
Olive oil, for drizzling
8 ounces cream cheese, softened
¾ cup sour cream
¼ cup mayonnaise
1 tablespoon apple cider vinegar

2 tablespoons chopped fresh chives
1 tablespoon chopped fresh parsley
¼ teaspoon salt, plus more as needed
¼ teaspoon freshly ground black pepper
¼ teaspoon garlic powder

1. Place the onion halves cut-side up into a baking pan. Drizzle with the olive oil. 2. To install the grill grate, position it flat on top of the heating element so it sits in place. 3. Place the pan on the grill grate, then close the hood. 4. Use the pellet scoop to pour pellets into the smoke box until filled to the top. Select SMOKER. Set grill temperature to 250°F and time to 1 hour. Select START/STOP to begin cooking. Cook until the onions are tender and have browned slightly. 5. Once cooked, remove from the smoker and let them cool for 1 hour. Chop into small pieces and set aside. 6. In a medium bowl, mix together the cream cheese, sour cream, mayonnaise, and apple cider vinegar. Fold in the chopped cooked onions, chives, parsley, salt, black pepper, and garlic powder. Mix to incorporate, then serve.

Fiesta Shrimp Salsa with Tortilla Chips

Prep Time: 20 minutes | Cook Time: 16 minutes | Serves: 4

1 poblano chile pepper, about 6 ounces
24 large shrimp (2⅓0 count), peeled and deveined, tails removed
Extra-virgin olive oil
2 medium tomatoes, seeded and finely diced (about 1 cup)
1 small Fresno chile pepper, seeded and minced
1 jalapeño chile pepper, seeded and minced
¼ cup finely diced red onion

1 large garlic clove, minced
3 tablespoons fresh lime juice
½ teaspoon kosher salt
½ teaspoon freshly ground black pepper
½ cup chopped fresh cilantro leaves
Tortilla chips

1. To install grill grate, position it flat on top of the heating element so it sits in place, then close hood. Use pellet scoop to pour pellets into smoke box until filled to top. 2. Select GRILL. Select WOODFIRE FLAVOR. Set grill temperature to LO. Set the time to 12 minutes. Select START/STOP to begin preheating. 3. When unit beeps to signify it has preheated and ADD FOOD displays, open hood and place the poblano on the grill grate. Close hood and grill for 12 minutes, flipping halfway through. 4. Transfer the grilled poblano to a medium bowl and cover it with plastic wrap to retain the steam. Allow it to sit for approximately 10 minutes. Then, remove and discard the charred skin, stem, and seeds, and finely dice the poblano into ¼-inch pieces. Return the diced poblano to the bowl. 5. Increase the temperature of the grill to high heat. Pat the shrimp dry with paper towels and lightly brush them all over with oil. Grill the shrimp until firm to the touch and just turning opaque in the center, 2 to 4 minutes, turning once. Remove from the grill and cut into ¼-inch pieces. 6. Add the shrimp, 1 tablespoon oil, the tomatoes, the Fresno and jalapeño chiles, the onion, garlic, lime juice, salt, and pepper to the bowl with the poblano. Toss to mix well. Cover and refrigerate for at least 1 hour or up to 4 hours. 7. Just before serving, stir in the cilantro. Serve the salsa immediately with tortilla chips.

Easy Grilled Pineapple and Peaches

Prep Time: 20 minutes | Cook Time: 10 minutes | Serves: 4

1 whole pineapple
2 whole peaches
½ cup freshly squeezed orange juice or water
1 tablespoon freshly squeezed lemon juice

2 tablespoons light brown sugar
1 tablespoon honey
½ teaspoon salt

1. Prepare the pineapple. Cut off the top and bottom ends. Set the pineapple upright and make a cut down the side. Rotate the fruit slightly and continue to cut off the entire rind, removing any dark spiny parts. Place the pineapple on its side and cut it into 1-inch-thick disks. 2. Prepare the peaches. Rinse and dry the peaches. Using a small paring knife, halve it around the pit. Remove the halves from the pit. 3. Make the glaze. In a small saucepan over low heat, combine the orange juice, lemon juice, brown sugar, honey, and salt. Cook until the sugar melts. 4. To install grill grate, position it flat on top of the heating element so it sits in place, then close hood. Use pellet scoop to pour pellets into smoke box until filled to top. 5. Select GRILL. Select WOODFIRE FLAVOR. Set grill temperature to LO. Set the time to 4 minutes. Select START/STOP to begin preheating. 6. When unit beeps to signify it has preheated and ADD FOOD displays, open hood and place the peach halves and pineapple slices on the grill grate. Close hood and grill for 4 minutes, flipping halfway through. 7. Brush a small amount of glaze over the fruit and grill for 5 to 6 minutes more, turning every 1 or 2 minutes, until softened and golden brown, being careful that the fruit does not burn. Remove from the grill. 8. Let the fruit rest for 5 minutes before serving, diced or as-is.

Grilled Flatbread

Prep Time: 40 minutes | Cook Time: 16 minutes | Serves: 4

4 tablespoons (½ stick) butter
¾ cup water

2 cups all-purpose flour, divided
1 teaspoon salt

1. Make the dough. In small bowl, combine the butter and water. Microwave on high for 45 seconds to melt. In a large bowl, mix together 1¾ cups of flour, the salt, and the butter-water mixture until it forms a sticky ball. Sprinkle a work surface with some of the remaining flour. Knead the dough for 1 to 2 minutes until smooth. Return the dough to the large bowl, cover, and let rest at room temperature for 30 minutes. 2. Prepare the flatbread. Cut the dough into 8 uniform pieces. On a floured surface, press the dough. Using a rolling pin, roll the dough into a 6-inch circle. Repeat with the remaining pieces. 3. To install the grill grate, position it flat on top of the heating element so it sits in place. 4. Select the BAKE function. Adjust the temperature to 375°F and time to 4 minutes. Select START/STOP to begin preheating. 5. When preheating is complete, open the hood and place the flatbread on the grate. You may cook them in batches. Once the hood is closed, cooking will begin and the timer will start counting down, flipping halfway through. Bake until large bubbles begin to form and it turns slightly golden brown. Repeat with the remaining flatbread pieces. Serve immediately.

Cheese Bacon Egg Pizza

Prep Time: 20 minutes | Cook Time: 2 minutes | Serves: 2

1 (11-ounce) can refrigerated thin-crust pizza dough
All-purpose flour, for dusting
8 ounces fresh mozzarella, torn into small pieces

1½ ounces goat cheese, crumbled
4 bacon slices
4 large eggs

1. On a lightly floured work surface, roll out the dough to a 12- to 13-inch diameter. 2. Top with the mozzarella and goat cheeses and the bacon. 3. Put the pizza on parchment paper on a baking pan and crack the eggs on top. 4. To install the grill grate, position it flat on top of the heating element so it sits in place. 5. Select the BAKE function. Adjust the temperature to 650°F and time to 2 minutes. Select START/STOP to begin preheating. 6. When preheating is complete, open the hood and place the baking pan on the grate. Once the hood is closed, cooking will begin and the timer will start counting down. 7. Bake until the cheese is melted, the egg whites are set but the yolks are still runny, and the bacon is cooked. Serve immediately.

Easy Caprese Salad

Prep Time: 35 minutes | Cook Time: 0 minutes | Serves: 4

3 ripe tomatoes
2 (8-ounce) balls fresh mozzarella cheese
12 large fresh basil leaves
2 tablespoons balsamic vinegar (optional)

¼ cup olive oil
Salt
Black pepper

1. Cut the tomatoes into ¼-inch slices (about 4 slices per tomato). Cut the cheese into ¼-inch slices (about 6 slices per cheese ball). Wash and dry each basil leaf. 2. Assemble the salad. Lay the tomatoes on a large serving platter. Place 1 basil leaf on top of each tomato slice. Lay 1 slice of cheese on top, then drizzle each portion with vinegar (if using) and olive oil. Season with salt and pepper to taste. 3. Let the salad sit in the refrigerator to season for 30 minutes before serving.

Homemade Caesar Salad

Prep Time: 15 minutes | Cook Time: 0 minutes | Serves: 4

1 large egg yolk, at room temperature
3 garlic cloves, peeled
3 anchovy fillets
2 tablespoons freshly squeezed lemon juice
1 tablespoon red wine vinegar
4 tablespoons grated Parmesan cheese, divided

1 teaspoon dried mustard
½ teaspoon salt
½ teaspoon black pepper
⅓ cup olive oil
1 head romaine lettuce
2 cups unseasoned croutons

1. Make the dressing. In a blender, combine the egg yolk, anchovies, lemon juice, garlic, vinegar, 2 tablespoons of Parmesan cheese, the dried mustard, salt, pepper, and olive oil. Blend on low speed until smooth. Transfer the dressing to a small container and refrigerate. 2. Assemble the salad. Clean and rinse the romaine leaves and chop into bite-size pieces. Place the lettuce in a large salad bowl and add the croutons. 3. Toss. Pour the dressing over the salad and toss to coat and combine. Sprinkle with the remaining 2 tablespoons of Parmesan cheese. Serve immediately.

Simple Smoked Eggs

Prep Time: 10 minutes | Cook Time: 30 minutes | Serves: 12

12 hardboiled eggs, peeled and rinsed

1. To install the grill grate, position it flat on top of the heating element so it sits in place. 2. Place the eggs on the grill grate, then close the hood. 3. Use the pellet scoop to pour pellets into the smoke box until filled to the top. Select SMOKER. Set grill temperature to 120°F and time to 30 minutes. Select START/STOP to begin cooking. They will begin to take on a slight brown sheen. 4. Remove the eggs and refrigerate for at least 30 minutes before serving. Refrigerate any leftovers in an airtight container for 1 or 2 weeks.

Cheese Pulled Pork Potato Skins

Prep Time: 15 minutes | Cook Time: 3 hours | Serves: 4

5 medium-size russet potatoes
2 tablespoons olive oil
Kosher salt
Freshly ground black pepper
3 to 4 cups pulled pork

¾ cup barbecue sauce of choice
2 cups shredded cheddar cheese
Sour cream, for serving (optional)
Pickled jalapeños peppers, for serving (optional)

1. Brush all sides of the potatoes with olive oil and season with salt and black pepper. 2. To install the grill grate, position it flat on top of the heating element so it sits in place. 3. Place the potatoes on the grill grate, then close the hood. 4. Use the pellet scoop to pour pellets into the smoke box until filled to the top. Select SMOKER. Set grill temperature to 250°F and time to 2½ hours. Select START/STOP to begin cooking. 5. Remove the potatoes and cut them in half lengthwise. Let them cool slightly. 6. Using a spoon, remove most of the potato flesh from the skins. (You can discard this or save it for another recipe.) Distribute the pulled pork evenly among each potato skin, then drizzle barbecue sauce over them and sprinkle shredded cheese on top. 7. Place the potato skins back in the smoker (still at 250°F) for 30 minutes. 8. Remove from the grill and top with sour cream and pickled jalapeños (if using).

Shrimp Kebabs with Rémoulade

Prep Time: 15 minutes | Cook Time: 4 minutes | Serves: 6

2 pounds extra-large shrimp (16/20 count), peeled and deveined, tails left on
Sauce:
½ cup mayonnaise
1 tablespoon drained capers, minced
1 tablespoon sweet pickle relish
1 tablespoon finely chopped fresh tarragon leaves
2 teaspoons minced shallot

Extra-virgin olive oil
Kosher salt and freshly ground black pepper

1 teaspoon tarragon vinegar or white wine vinegar
1 teaspoon minced garlic
½ teaspoon Dijon mustard
¼ teaspoon paprika
⅛ teaspoon kosher salt

1. In a small bowl, whisk together the sauce ingredients. If not using right away, cover and refrigerate for up to 24 hours. 2. Have ready 12 metal or bamboo skewers. If using bamboo, soak in water for at least 30 minutes. 3. To install grill grate, position it flat on top of the heating element so it sits in place, then close hood. Use pellet scoop to pour pellets into smoke box until filled to top. 4. Select GRILL. Select WOODFIRE FLAVOR. Set grill temperature to HI. Set the time to 4 minutes. Select START/STOP to begin preheating. 5. Skewer 4 shrimps onto each skewer, bending each shrimp almost in half to allow the skewer to pass through it twice, once near the head and once near the tail. Lightly brush the shrimp all over with oil and season with salt and pepper. 6. When unit beeps to signify it has preheated and ADD FOOD displays, open hood and place the shrimp on the grill grate. Close hood and grill for 4 minutes, flipping halfway through. 7. Remove from the grill and serve warm with the sauce.

Hot Smoked Almonds

Prep Time: 10 minutes | Cook Time: 3 hours | Serves: 10

2 pounds raw natural almonds
About 1½ tablespoons hot sauce

1 tablespoon of your favorite barbecue rub, or to taste (optional)

1. In a medium bowl, toss the almonds, hot sauce, and rub (if using) together until the nuts are well coated with the sauce and rub. Pour into a baking pan in an even layer. 2. To install the grill grate, position it flat on top of the heating element so it sits in place. 3. Place the pan on the grill grate, then close the hood. 4. Use the pellet scoop to pour pellets into the smoke box until filled to the top. Select SMOKER. Set grill temperature to 225°F and time to 3 hours. Select START/STOP to begin cooking. Smoke until the nuts are crisp. 5. Let cool completely and store in an airtight container; they will keep at room temperature for up to a week but, believe me, they won't last that long! They also will freeze nicely for a couple of months.

Spicy Garlic Shrimp

Prep Time: 30 minutes | Cook Time: 6 minutes | Serves: 4

20 jumbo shrimp (11/15 count), peeled and deveined, tails left on
Marinade:
¼ cup extra-virgin olive oil
2 tablespoons fresh lemon juice
2 tablespoons finely chopped fresh Italian parsley leaves and stems
2 teaspoons dried oregano
1½ teaspoons minced garlic

1 tablespoon fine dried bread crumbs

1 teaspoon finely grated lemon zest
½ teaspoon kosher salt
¼ teaspoon freshly ground black pepper
¼ teaspoon crushed red pepper flakes

1. In a small bowl, whisk together the marinade ingredients. Place the shrimp in a large, resealable plastic bag and pour in the marinade. Press the air out of the bag and seal tightly. Turn the bag to distribute the marinade, place in a bowl, and refrigerate for 30 minutes to 1 hour, turning occasionally. 2. Have ready 4 medium (about 10 inches long) or 20 small (about 4 inches long) metal or bamboo skewers. If using bamboo, soak in water for at least 30 minutes. 3. To install grill grate, position it flat on top of the heating element so it sits in place, then close hood. Use pellet scoop to pour pellets into smoke box until filled to top. 4. Select GRILL. Select WOODFIRE FLAVOR. Set grill temperature to HI. Set the time to 6 minutes. Select START/STOP to begin preheating. 5. Remove the shrimp from the bag and discard the marinade. Thread the shrimp onto the skewers, either 2 shrimp per skewer as hors d'oeuvres or 5 shrimp per skewer as appetizers, bending each shrimp almost in half so the skewer passes through it twice, near the head and near the tail. Sprinkle the shrimp evenly on both sides with the bread crumbs. 6. When unit beeps to signify it has preheated and ADD FOOD displays, open hood and place the shrimp on the grill grate. Close hood and grill for 6 minutes, flipping halfway through. 7. Remove from the grill and serve warm.

Peach and Blue Cheese Bruschetta

Prep Time: 10 minutes | Cook Time: 8 minutes | Serves: 4

4 ounces cream cheese, softened
2 tablespoons granulated sugar
1 tablespoon fresh thyme leaves
4 firm but ripe peaches

8 slices Italian or French bread, each about ½ inch thick
Extra-virgin olive oil
4 ounces blue cheese, crumbled (scant 1 cup)
3 tablespoons honey

1. To install grill grate, position it flat on top of the heating element so it sits in place, then close hood. Use pellet scoop to pour pellets into smoke box until filled to top. 2. Select GRILL. Select WOODFIRE FLAVOR. Set grill temperature to LO. Set the time to 8 minutes. Select START/STOP to begin preheating. 3. Stir together the cream cheese, sugar, and thyme until blended. Set aside. Cut each peach in half through the stem end and discard the pit. Lightly brush the peach halves and bread slices on both sides with oil. 4. When unit beeps to signify it has preheated and ADD FOOD displays, open hood and place the peach halves on the grill grate. Close hood and grill for 8 minutes, flipping halfway through. During the last 1 minute of grilling time, toast the bread slices in the grill, turning once. Remove the peaches and bread from the grill. 5. Spread each bread slice with an equal amount of the cream cheese mixture. Cut the peach halves into ¼-inch-thick slices. Distribute the peach slices evenly among the bread slices, slightly overlapping them. Sprinkle blue cheese over the peaches and drizzle honey on top. Serve immediately.

Filet Mignon Crostini

Prep Time: 20 minutes | Cook Time: 13 minutes | Serves: 12

3 filet mignon steaks, each about 8 ounces and 1½ inches thick
1 tablespoon extra-virgin olive oil
Crostini:
1 baguette, cut into 25 slices, each about ½ inch thick
Extra-virgin olive oil
Cream:
⅓ cup sour cream
3 tablespoons prepared horseradish
¼ teaspoon kosher salt

1½ teaspoons kosher salt
¾ teaspoon freshly ground black pepper

2 garlic cloves

½ teaspoon freshly ground black pepper
Balsamic Onion Jam
1 bunch fresh chives, chopped (optional)

1. Brush the steaks on both sides with the oil, then season on both sides with the salt and pepper. Let stand at room temperature for 15 to 30 minutes before grilling. 2. To install grill grate, position it flat on top of the heating element so it sits in place, then close hood. Use pellet scoop to pour pellets into smoke box until filled to top. 3. Select GRILL. Select WOODFIRE FLAVOR. Set grill temperature to HI. Set the time to minute. Select START/STOP to begin preheating. 4. Lightly brush one side of each baguette slice with oil. 5. When unit beeps to signify it has preheated and ADD FOOD displays, open hood and place the baguette slices on the grill grate. Close hood and grill for 1 minute. 6. Remove from the grill, let cool, and rub the grilled side lightly with the garlic. 7. Combine the cream ingredients in a small bowl. Cover and refrigerate until ready to use. 8. Grill the steaks over high heat, until cooked to your desired doneness, 12 to 14 minutes for medium rare, turning once. Remove from the grill and let rest for 3 to 5 minutes. Cut the steaks across the grain into ¼-inch-thick slices. 9. Spread a layer of jam on each toasted baguette slice. Place a slice of meat on the jam and top with a small dollop of the cream. Sprinkle with the chives, if desired.

Grilled Bacon-Wrapped Jalapeño Poppers

Prep Time: 35 minutes | Cook Time: 25 minutes | Serves: 4

8 small to medium jalapeño peppers
1 (8-ounce) brick Colby-Jack cheese, grated

8 thick-cut bacon slices
2 tablespoons barbecue rub of choice

1. Prepare the peppers. Make a slit lengthwise down one side of each jalapeño and use a small sharp knife or spoon to remove the seeds. Fill the inside of each pepper with an equal amount of Colby-Jack cheese. Lay out the bacon slices on a work surface and place 1 jalapeño on the end of each slice. Roll the bacon over the jalapeño, covering it completely. Sprinkle each wrapped pepper with barbecue rub, coating all sides thoroughly. Secure the loose end of the bacon with a toothpick and place the peppers on a plate. Refrigerate for 30 minutes. 2. To install grill grate, position it flat on top of the heating element so it sits in place, then close hood. Use pellet scoop to pour pellets into smoke box until filled to top. 3. Select GRILL. Select WOODFIRE FLAVOR. Set grill temperature to LO. Set the time to 25 minutes. Select START/STOP to begin preheating. 4. When unit beeps to signify it has preheated and ADD FOOD displays, open hood and place the poppers on the grill grate. Close hood and grill for 25 minutes. Grill until the bacon is fully cooked. Do not turn or flip the poppers while cooking. 5. Remove from the heat and let rest for 5 minutes before serving.

Crispy Russet Potato Fries

Prep Time: 10 minutes | Cook Time: 19 minutes | Serves: 4

2 large russet potatoes
¼ cup olive oil
¼ cup salt

2 teaspoons black pepper
2 teaspoons garlic powder
2 teaspoons onion powder

1. Wash the potatoes well and dry with a paper towel. Halve each potato and place the potato halves, cut-side down, on a work surface. Cut each half lengthwise into ½-inch planks. Cut each plank into ½-inch fries. Put the fries on a large microwave-safe plate and pour the olive oil over the potatoes. Mix until coated. Microwave on high power for 1 minute, or until the potatoes still have a slightly firm texture. Cool completely. 2. In a small bowl, stir together the salt, pepper, garlic powder, and onion powder. Sprinkle the seasoning over the fries and toss to coat. Cover and let sit in the seasoning at room temperature for 15 minutes. 3. To install the grill grate, position it flat on top of the heating element so it sits in place. Oil the grill grate. 4. Select the ROAST function. Adjust the temperature to 375°F and time to 18 minutes. Select START/STOP to begin preheating. 5. When preheating is complete, open the hood and place the fries in a single layer on the grill grate. Once the hood is closed, cooking will begin and the timer will begin counting down, turning with a spatula every 3 to 4 minutes. Remove from the grill grate and serve immediately.

Spicy Chicken Skewers with Honey-Lime Cream

Prep Time: 30 minutes | Cook Time: 8 minutes | Serves: 6

Paste:
1 habanero or Scotch bonnet chile pepper
1 cup loosely packed fresh cilantro leaves and tender stems
½ cup extra-virgin olive oil
4 scallions (white and light green parts only), roughly chopped
2 tablespoons finely chopped, peeled fresh ginger
2 tablespoons granulated sugar
1 tablespoon fresh lime juice

1 tablespoon ground allspice
6 medium garlic cloves, peeled
2 teaspoons kosher salt
1 teaspoon freshly ground black pepper
6 boneless, skinless chicken breast halves, each 6 to 8 ounces, trimmed of excess fat
Honey-Lime Cream

1. Both habanero and Scotch bonnet chiles are extremely hot, so it's essential to wear rubber or plastic gloves to protect your skin when handling them. Avoid touching your face or any other body part after handling the chiles, as this can cause a burning sensation. Remove and discard the chile's stem, then cut away and discard the hot whitish veins and seeds. Place the remaining part of the chile in the bowl of a food processor. Add the rest of the paste ingredients and process until smooth. 2. Remove the tenders from the chicken breasts. Cut the chicken breasts lengthwise into even strips ½ to ¾ inch wide. Place the chicken strips and tenders in a large, sealable plastic bag, then add the paste using a spoon. Massage the paste into the chicken until evenly coated. Remove any excess air from the bag before sealing it tightly. Place in the refrigerator and marinate for 2 to 3 hours. 3. Have ready 8 to 12 metal or bamboo skewers. If using bamboo, soak in water for at least 30 minutes. 4. To install grill grate, position it flat on top of the heating element so it sits in place, then close hood. Use pellet scoop to pour pellets into smoke box until filled to top. 5. Select GRILL. Select WOODFIRE FLAVOR. Set grill temperature to HI. Set the time to 8 minutes. Select START/STOP to begin preheating. 6. Put on gloves again, then thread the chicken strips lengthwise onto the skewers, passing the skewer through the meat at least twice and keeping the skewer in the center of the strip. (If you don't wear gloves, be sure to wash your hands thoroughly after this step.) 7. When unit beeps to signify it has preheated and ADD FOOD displays, open hood and place the skewers on the grill grate. Close hood and grill for 8 minutes, flipping halfway through. 8. Remove from the grill and serve warm with the honey-lime cream.

Sweet & Sour Chicken Wings

Prep Time: 10 minutes | Cook Time: 2 hours | Serves: 8

1¼ cup peach jelly or preserves
½ cup bourbon
½ cup honey
¼ cup soy sauce
¼ cup balsamic vinegar

Kosher salt
Freshly ground black pepper
Pinch red pepper flakes
5 pounds jumbo split chicken wings

1. In a bowl, combine the peach jelly, bourbon, honey, soy sauce, balsamic vinegar, salt, black pepper, and red pepper flakes and whisk until evenly mixed. 2. Pat the chicken wings dry with paper towels and put them in a gallon-size plastic bag. Add 1 cup of the peach-bourbon mixture to the bag and massage the bag until the wings are evenly coated. Marinate in the refrigerator for at least 1 hour or overnight. Store the remaining sauce in a sealed container in the refrigerator. 3. To install the grill grate, position it flat on top of the heating element so it sits in place. 4. Place the wings on the grill grate, then close the hood. 5. Use the pellet scoop to pour pellets into the smoke box until filled to the top. Select SMOKER. Set grill temperature to 250°F and time to 2 hours. Select START/STOP to begin cooking, flipping halfway through. 6. Brush some of the reserved peach bourbon sauce on the wings during the last 15 minutes of cooking and serve the wings with the remaining sauce on the side.

Cheesy Crab and Artichoke Dip

Prep Time: 10 minutes | Cook Time: 2 hours | Serves: 8

8 ounces cream cheese
½ cup mayonnaise
½ cup sour cream
3½ tablespoons Cajun or seafood seasoning
2 tablespoons Worcestershire sauce
2 tablespoons freshly squeezed lemon juice

Dash hot sauce of choice (optional)
2 cups shredded Monterey Jack cheese
1 cup shredded Parmesan cheese
1 (14-ounce) jar marinated artichokes, drained and chopped
1-pound canned crabmeat
Tortilla chips or crostini, for serving

1. In a large bowl, combine the cream cheese, mayonnaise, sour cream, Cajun seasoning, Worcestershire sauce, lemon juice, and hot sauce (if using). Mix with a spoon or hand mixer until evenly combined. 2. Add the cheeses, artichokes, and crabmeat. Gently fold everything together with a spoon. 3. Transfer the dip to a baking pan. 4. To install the grill grate, position it flat on top of the heating element so it sits in place. 5. Place the pan on the grill grate, then close the hood. 6. Use the pellet scoop to pour pellets into the smoke box until filled to the top. Select SMOKER. Set grill temperature to 250°F and time to 2 hours. Select START/STOP to begin cooking. 7. Remove from the grill, let cool slightly, and serve with tortilla chips or crostini.

Cheese Jalapeño Stuffed Mushrooms

Prep Time: 15 minutes | Cook Time: 25 minutes | Serves: 8

6 slices bacon, cooked and crumbled
8 ounces cream cheese, at room temperature
2 jalapeño peppers, minced
1 cup shredded cheese of choice

Kosher salt
Freshly ground black pepper
1-pound baby portobello mushrooms, washed and dried

1. In a large bowl, put the bacon, cream cheese, jalapeños, shredded cheese, salt, and black pepper. Stir until evenly combined. 2. Remove the stems from the mushrooms. 3. To install grill grate, position it flat on top of the heating element so it sits in place, then close hood. Use pellet scoop to pour pellets into smoke box until filled to top. 4. Select GRILL. Select WOODFIRE FLAVOR. Set grill temperature to LO. Set the time to 25 minutes. Select START/STOP to begin preheating. 5. Divide the filling into each mushroom cap. 6. When unit beeps to signify it has preheated and ADD FOOD displays, open hood and place he stuffed mushrooms on the grill grate. Close hood and grill for 25 minutes, flipping halfway through. 7. Remove from the grill and serve right away.

Baked Buffalo Chicken Nachos

Prep Time: 10 minutes | Cook Time: 15 minutes | Serves: 6

8 ounces tortilla chips, divided
2 cups cooked, shredded chicken, divided
3 cups shredded cheddar cheese, divided

½ cup Buffalo sauce
½ cup ranch dressing

1. To install the grill grate, position it flat on top of the heating element so it sits in place. 2. Select the BAKE function. Adjust the temperature to 375°F and time to 15 minutes. Select START/STOP to begin preheating. 3. Put half of the chips in a single layer in a baking pan. Arrange half of the shredded chicken followed by half of the cheese over the chips. 4. Next, layer the remaining chips over the chicken and cheese, and top with the remaining chicken and cheese. 5. When preheating is complete, open the hood and place the pan on the grate. Once the hood is closed, cooking will begin and the timer will start counting down. 6. Before serving, drizzle the Buffalo sauce and ranch dressing over the top.

Roasted Chipotle-Rubbed Chicken Wings

Prep Time: 10 minutes | Cook Time: 1 hour | Serves: 8

5 pounds jumbo split chicken wings
2 tablespoons chipotle seasoning
2 tablespoons baking powder
1 tablespoon dry mustard
1 tablespoon garlic powder

1 tablespoon chili powder
½ tablespoon cumin
Kosher salt
Freshly ground black pepper

1. Pat the wings dry really well with paper towels and put them in a large bowl. 2. In a smaller bowl, mix together the chipotle seasoning, baking powder, dry mustard, garlic powder, chili powder, cumin, and a pinch each of salt and pepper, then add to the chicken wings. Toss until the wings are evenly coated. 3. To install the grill grate, position it flat on top of the heating element so it sits in place. 4. Select the ROAST function. Adjust the temperature to 425°F and time to 1 hour. Select START/STOP to begin preheating. 5. When preheating is complete, open the hood and place the chicken wings on the grill grate. Once the hood is closed, cooking will begin and the timer will begin counting down. Flip them halfway through. Serve right away.

Hot and Sweet Chicken Wings

Prep Time: 10 minutes | Cook Time: 18 minutes | Serves: 8

20 chicken wings, about 3 pounds total
Marinade:
½ cup ketchup
¼ cup balsamic vinegar
2 tablespoons packed dark brown sugar
4 teaspoons garlic powder
4 teaspoons Worcestershire sauce

Extra-virgin olive oil

1 tablespoon hot-pepper sauce
2 teaspoons Dijon mustard
2 teaspoons paprika
2 teaspoons pure chile powder

1. In a bowl, whisk together the marinade ingredients. Put the wings in a large, resealable plastic bag and pour in the marinade. Press the air out of the bag and seal tightly. Turn the bag to distribute the marinade, place in a bowl, and refrigerate for 4 to 6 hours, turning the bag occasionally. 2. To install grill grate, position it flat on top of the heating element so it sits in place, then close hood. Use pellet scoop to pour pellets into smoke box until filled to top. 3. Select GRILL. Select WOODFIRE FLAVOR. Set grill temperature to LO. Set the time to 6 minutes. Select START/STOP to begin preheating. 4. When unit beeps to signify it has preheated and ADD FOOD displays, open hood. Remove the chicken wings from the bag and discard the marinade. Lightly brush the wings with oil and place on the grill grate. Close hood and grill for 6 minutes, flipping halfway through. 5. Adjust to high heat and cook for 12 minutes more, turning once or twice. Remove from the grill and serve warm.

Savory Turkey Meatballs

Prep Time: 30 minutes | Cook Time: 15 minutes | Serves: 10

Meatballs:
1½ pounds ground turkey, preferably thigh meat
¼ cup finely chopped fresh cilantro leaves
2 scallions, minced
1 tablespoon soy sauce
1 tablespoon peeled, grated fresh ginger
Sauce:
½ cup rice vinegar
¼ cup fresh lime juice
¼ cup granulated sugar
1 tablespoon finely chopped fresh cilantro leaves

2 teaspoons hot chile-garlic sauce, such as Sriracha
2 garlic cloves, minced
1 teaspoon ground coriander
1 teaspoon kosher salt
Vegetable oil

2 teaspoons minced red jalapeño chile pepper
2 teaspoons peeled, grated fresh ginger
1 teaspoon kosher salt
1 garlic clove, minced

1. In a medium bowl, combine all of the meatball ingredients except oil and mix gently until evenly distributed. With wet hands, form into uniform balls, each about 1½ inches in diameter. Cover with plastic wrap and refrigerate for at least 1 hour. 2. In a small saucepan over medium-high heat, combine the vinegar, lime juice, and sugar. Bring to a boil and cook until the sugar dissolves and the liquid is reduced by one-third, about 5 minutes, stirring occasionally. Transfer the mixture to a bowl and stir in the remaining sauce ingredients. Let cool completely. 3. To install the grill grate, position it flat on top of the heating element so it sits in place. 4. Select the ROAST function. Adjust the temperature to 400°F and time to 10 minutes. Select START/STOP to begin preheating. 5. When preheating is complete, open the hood. Lightly brush the meatballs with oil and place on the grill grate. Once the hood is closed, cooking will begin and the timer will begin counting down, turning two or three times. Remove from the grill and serve warm with the sauce.

Cheesy Steak & Black Beans Nachos

Prep Time: 30 minutes | Cook Time: 11 minutes | Serves: 12

1½ pounds skirt steak, ½ to ¾ inch thick, trimmed of excess surface fat, cut with the grain into 12-inch-long pieces
1 bag (12 ounces) tortilla chips
1 can (15 ounces) black beans, rinsed and drained
Paste:
1 tablespoon extra-virgin olive oil
1 tablespoon minced garlic
1 teaspoon pure chile powder
1 teaspoon packed light brown sugar

2 cups shredded Monterey Jack cheese (8 ounces)
2 cups shredded sharp cheddar cheese (8 ounces)
Tomato-Avocado Salsa

½ teaspoon kosher salt
½ teaspoon chipotle chile powder
¼ teaspoon ground cumin

1. In a small bowl, mix together the paste ingredients. Brush the paste on both sides of the steak pieces. Let the steak stand at room temperature for 15 to 30 minutes before grilling. 2. To install grill grate, position it flat on top of the heating element so it sits in place, then close hood. Use pellet scoop to pour pellets into smoke box until filled to top. 3. Select GRILL. Select WOODFIRE FLAVOR. Set grill temperature to HI. Set the time to 6 minutes. Select START/STOP to begin preheating. 4. When unit beeps to signify it has preheated and ADD FOOD displays, open hood and place the steak pieces on the grill grate. Close hood and grill for 6 minutes, flipping halfway through. 5. Remove from the grill and let rest for 3 to 5 minutes. Cut the steak across the grain into bite-sized pieces. 6. Layer half of the tortilla chips, steak, black beans, and cheddar and Monterey Jack cheeses on a large sheet pan. Place the pan on the grill grate and cook on high heat until the cheese is melted, about 5 minutes. Remove from the grill and serve immediately with the salsa. Repeat with the remaining ingredients on a second large sheet pan.

Grilled Watermelon Wedges with Feta

Prep Time: 10 minutes | Cook Time: 8 minutes | Serves: 4

2 tablespoons canola oil
1 (3-pound) watermelon (seedless preferred)
¼ cup balsamic vinegar

1 cup feta cheese crumbles
12 fresh mint leaves, chopped
Grated zest of 1 lemon

1. To install grill grate, position it flat on top of the heating element so it sits in place, then close hood. Use pellet scoop to pour pellets into smoke box until filled to top. 2. Select GRILL. Select WOODFIRE FLAVOR. Set grill temperature to HI. Set the time to 8 minutes. Select START/STOP to begin preheating. 3. Slice the watermelon into 2-inch-thick rounds. Slice each round into 4 wedges. 4. When unit beeps to signify it has preheated and ADD FOOD displays, open hood and place the watermelon slices on the grill grate. Close hood and grill for 8 minutes, flipping halfway through. 5. Transfer the watermelon slices to a platter and drizzle them lightly with the vinegar. Sprinkle on the feta crumbles and top with the mint and lemon zest.

Cheese Sausage-Stuffed Jalapeños

Prep Time: 20 minutes | Cook Time: 25 minutes | Serves: 8

1 pound loose ground Italian sausage
8 ounces cream cheese
2 cups shredded cheddar cheese

Kosher salt
Freshly ground black pepper
12 to 14 jalapeño peppers

1. In a medium skillet, cook the sausage over medium heat for 5 to 7 minutes, breaking it apart as it cooks. Remove the skillet from the heat and add the cream cheese, cheddar cheese, salt, and black pepper. Stir until melted together, then set aside to let this mixture cool. 2. Cut the jalapeños in half lengthwise and use a spoon to scrape out the seeds and white parts out of each. 3. To install the grill grate, position it flat on top of the heating element so it sits in place. 4. Select the ROAST function. Adjust the temperature to 350°F and time to 20 minutes. Select START/STOP to begin preheating. 5. Stuff the jalapeños with the sausage-and-cheese filling. 6. When preheating is complete, open the hood and place the stuffed jalapeños on the grill grate. Once the hood is closed, cooking will begin and the timer will begin counting down. 7. Serve immediately.

Roasted Garlic Potatoes

Prep Time: 20 minutes | Cook Time: 30 minutes | Serves: 4

4 large red-skinned potatoes
1 onion, diced
2 garlic cloves, minced

3 tablespoons olive oil
2 teaspoons salt
2 teaspoons black pepper

1.Wash the potatoes well and dry with a paper towel. Cut each potato into 1-inch cubes (8 to 10 cubes per potato). Place the potatoes in a large bowl and add the onion, garlic, olive oil, salt, and pepper. Toss to coat and combine. 2. Cut 2 (15-by-12-inch) pieces of heavy-duty aluminum foil and stack the pieces. Put the seasoned potatoes into the center of the foil pieces and fold the corners together, forming a tightly sealed square. 3. To install the grill grate, position it flat on top of the heating element so it sits in place. 4. Select the ROAST function. Adjust the temperature to 425°F and time to 30 minutes. Select START/STOP to begin preheating. 5. When preheating is complete, open the hood. Oil the grill grate, then place the foil pack of potatoes, folded-side up, on the grate. Once the hood is closed, cooking will begin and the timer will begin counting down. 6. Remove the potatoes from the grill and let rest for 5 minutes before serving.

Chapter 9 Rubs, Brines, Marinades, and Sauces

Chimichurri Sauce

Prep Time: 10 minutes | Cook Time: 0 minutes | Serves: 6

1 bunch fresh parsley, stemmed, washed, and chopped
8 garlic cloves, peeled
¾ cup olive oil
⅓ cup red wine vinegar

Juice of 1 lemon
1 teaspoon red pepper flakes
½ teaspoon salt
½ teaspoon black pepper

1. Make the chimichurri. In a food processor, combine the parsley, garlic, olive oil, vinegar, lemon juice, red pepper flakes, salt, and black pepper. Process on high speed for 2 to 3 minutes until the mixture is finely chopped. 2. Marinate. Transfer the chimichurri to a bowl and cover. Let sit at room temperature for 2 to 3 hours before serving.

Blood Orange Sauce

Prep Time: 10 minutes | Cook Time: 10 minutes | Serves: 1 cup

Juice of 2 blood oranges
Juice of 2 large oranges, such as Valencia or Cara Cara
½ cup maple syrup
2 teaspoons bourbon
⅓ cup ketchup

2 tablespoons butter
2 teaspoons soy sauce
½ teaspoon mild chili powder
Pinch salt
Pinch freshly ground black pepper

1. In a medium saucepan over medium heat, combine the blood orange juice, other orange juice, and maple syrup. Simmer for 2 minutes, stirring often. 2. Add the bourbon and let the sauce simmer for 1 minute more, then add the ketchup, butter, soy sauce, chili powder, salt, and pepper. Reduce the heat to low and simmer for an additional 5 to 7 minutes. The sauce will start to thicken and take on the consistency of syrup. Remove from heat, cover, and keep warm. If making the sauce for later use, allow it to cool completely and store in the refrigerator for up to 1 week.

Flavorful Barbecue Sauce

Prep Time: 10 minutes | Cook Time: 5 minutes | Serves: 12

1½ cups ketchup
¾ cup unsweetened apple juice
¾ cup cider vinegar
3 tablespoons packed light brown sugar
3 tablespoons tomato paste
1½ tablespoons unsulfured molasses (not blackstrap)

1 tablespoon Worcestershire sauce
1½ teaspoons mustard powder
¾ teaspoon hot-pepper sauce
¾ teaspoon kosher salt
½ teaspoon freshly ground black pepper

In a medium, heavy saucepan whisk together all the ingredients. Place over medium heat on the stove and bring to a simmer. Cook for about 5 minutes, stirring occasionally. Set aside. (The sauce can be made up to 4 days ahead. Let cool completely, then cover and refrigerate. Warm gently before serving.)

Honey Pepper Rub

Prep Time: 5 minutes | Cook Time: 0 minutes | Makes: 1¾ cups

¼ cup honey powder
½ cup paprika
½ cup chili powder
1 tablespoon ground bee pollen (optional)
1 tablespoon garlic powder
1 tablespoon onion powder
1 tablespoon ground coriander

1 tablespoon ground dry mustard
1 tablespoon ground cumin
1 tablespoon freshly ground white pepper
1 tablespoon freshly ground black pepper
1 teaspoon ground cayenne pepper
1 tablespoon kosher salt
1 teaspoon ground celery seed

1. In a small bowl, combine the honey powder, paprika, chili powder, bee pollen (if using), garlic powder, onion powder, coriander, mustard, cumin, white pepper, black pepper, cayenne pepper, salt, and celery seed. 2. Apply evenly to all sides of meat 30 minutes to 3 hours before cooking.

Tangy Tomato Salsa

Prep Time: 10 minutes | Cook Time: 12 minutes | Serves: 4

8 Roma tomatoes
2 jalapeño peppers
1 garlic clove, peeled
¼ cup diced onion
¼ cup chopped fresh cilantro

2 teaspoons salt
1 teaspoon dried oregano
1 teaspoon freshly squeezed lime juice
½ teaspoon black pepper

1. To install the grill grate, position it flat on top of the heating element so it sits in place. 2. Select the GRILL function. Adjust the temperature to HI and time to 7 minutes. Select START/STOP to begin preheating. 3. Line a baking sheet with aluminum foil. Set aside. 4. Prepare the ingredients. Halve the tomatoes, then core them using a spoon. Halve the jalapeños lengthwise and remove the seeds and core. 5. Broil the vegetables. Put the tomatoes and jalapeños on the prepared baking sheet. 6. When preheating is complete, open the hood and place the baking sheet on the grate. Once the hood is closed, cooking will begin and the timer will start counting down. 7. Grill until the tomatoes and jalapeño just start to blacken. Turn them to the other side and add the garlic. Broil for about 5 minutes more, until both sides are about half blistered and black. Remove from the oven and let cool. 8. Make the salsa. Transfer the cooled vegetables and garlic to a food processor or blender. Add the onion, cilantro, salt, oregano, lime juice, and pepper. Blend until pureed, but do not overblend. You may need to add a bit of water if the salsa is too thick. Pour the salsa into a bowl, cover, and refrigerate for at least 2 hours so the flavors meld.

Homemade Barbecue Sauce

Prep Time: 10 minutes | Cook Time: 15 minutes | Makes 2¼ cups

¼ cup sugar
1 tablespoon salt
½ cup apple cider vinegar
2 cups ketchup
½ teaspoons cayenne pepper
1½ teaspoons garlic powder

1 teaspoon celery seed
1 teaspoon ground cumin
1 teaspoon chili powder
1 teaspoon black pepper
½ teaspoon liquid smoke
1 teaspoon freshly squeezed lemon juice

1. In a medium saucepan over medium heat, combine the sugar and salt. Pour in the vinegar and bring to a simmer. Lower the heat and simmer for 5 minutes. Stir in the ketchup, then stir in the cayenne, garlic powder, celery seed, cumin, chili powder, and black pepper. Add the liquid smoke and lemon juice. Simmer the sauce for 10 minutes more. 2. Remove from the heat, cover the pan, and let cool until the sauce can be funneled into a cleaned leftover ketchup bottle or jar.

Spicy Beef and Game Rub

Prep Time: 15 minutes | Cook Time: 1 minute | Makes: ½ cup

2 tablespoons whole peppercorns
1 tablespoon cumin seeds
1 tablespoon coriander seeds
2 tablespoons coarse, kosher, or sea salt

1 teaspoon granulated garlic
½ teaspoon smoked paprika
½ teaspoon cayenne pepper

1. In a small skillet over medium heat, toast the peppercorns, cumin seeds, and coriander seeds for 1 minute, or until fragrant. Shake the pan gently during the toasting process to avoid burning the spices. 2. Pour the toasted spices onto a plate and let them cool completely. Grind them in a spice grinder or use a mortar and pestle to pulverize them. 3. In a small bowl, mix up the ground spices, salt, granulated garlic, smoked paprika, and cayenne pepper. Use immediately or store in a closed container in the cupboard for up to a year.

Citrus Sauce

Prep Time: 10 minutes | Cook Time: 2 minutes | Makes: 2 cups

10 garlic cloves, smashed
1 tablespoon dried oregano
1 cup extra-virgin olive oil
½ cup freshly squeezed orange juice

Juice of 1½ limes
Juice of ½ lemon
1 tablespoon kosher salt
Stems of 1 bunch fresh cilantro

1. In a medium saucepan, heat the garlic and oregano in the oil over medium heat for 1 to 2 minutes or until fragrant. 2. Turn off the heat, let cool, and add the orange juice, lime juice, lemon juice, salt, and cilantro stems. Transfer to the bowl of a small food processor. Blend until the cilantro stems are finely chopped. Transfer to an airtight container. 3. Refrigerate until completely chilled before using and up to 1 week.

Asian-Style Marinade

Prep Time: 15 minutes | Cook Time: 15 minutes | Serves: 4

1 cup fresh cilantro leaves, finely chopped
3 garlic cloves, minced
2 limes, thinly sliced
1 jalapeño pepper, trimmed, seeded, and diced
¼ cup packed dark brown sugar
3 tablespoons canola oil

3 tablespoons soy sauce
3 tablespoons fish sauce
1 tablespoon toasted sesame oil
1 teaspoon ground coriander
1 teaspoon freshly ground black pepper

1. In a large stockpot over medium heat, combine the cilantro, garlic, limes, jalapeño, sugar, canola oil, soy sauce, fish sauce, sesame oil, coriander, and black pepper. Bring to a simmer and cook for 5 minutes. 2. Whisk to combine the ingredients, remove the marinade from the heat, and cool it completely in the refrigerator before using. 3. To use, in a large food-safe plastic bag, combine the meat and marinade. Remove as much air as possible from the bag and seal it. Refrigerate to marinate your meat for 24 hours for best results. Massage the marinade into the meat and turn the bag occasionally. 4. Remove the meat from the marinade and cook it according to the recipe's instructions.

Garlicky Brisket Rub

Prep Time: 5 minutes | Cook Time: 0 minutes | Makes: 1½ cups

½ cup kosher salt
½ cup granulated garlic

1/3 cup freshly ground black pepper
¼ cup sweet paprika (optional)

Combine all the ingredients and store in an airtight container in a cool, dry place.

Limeade Marinade

Prep Time: 3 minutes | Cook Time: 0 minutes | Makes: 2 cups

¾ cup extra-virgin olive oil
¾ cup tamari
6 ounces frozen limeade concentrate, thawed

2 tablespoons minced garlic
2 tablespoons chopped fresh rosemary

In a medium bowl, whisk all the ingredients together.

Tangy Brine

Prep Time: 10 minutes | Cook Time: 0 minutes | Makes: 8 cups

2 quarts low-sodium chicken broth
2 cups apple juice
½ cup olive oil
1 cup of your favorite barbecue spice rub, divided

½ cup sugar
¼ cup kosher salt
¼ cup Worcestershire sauce
2 cups (4 sticks) unsalted butter, melted

In a large bowl, whisk all the ingredients together until the sugar and salt dissolve. If using as an injection, load up your injector and give the pork all it will take. If brining, let the pork sit in it overnight and up to 2 days.

Cinnamon Spice Rub

Prep Time: 10 minutes | Cook Time: 0 minutes | Makes: ½ cup

2 tablespoons smoked paprika
2 tablespoons light brown sugar
1 tablespoon sesame seeds
1 tablespoon ground cinnamon
2 teaspoons ground cumin
2 teaspoons ground coriander

2 teaspoons kosher salt
1 teaspoon freshly ground black pepper
1 teaspoon ground ginger
1 teaspoon ground turmeric
½ teaspoon ground fenugreek

Combine all the ingredients and store in an airtight container in a cool, dry place. It will keep for a couple of months.

Herb Spice Rub

Prep Time: 5 minutes | Cook Time: 0 minutes | Serves: ¾ cup

2 tablespoons kosher salt
2 tablespoons freshly ground black pepper
2 tablespoons onion powder
2 tablespoons garlic powder
2 tablespoons paprika
1¼ teaspoons oregano

1¼ teaspoons dried thyme
1¼ teaspoons dried parsley
1 teaspoon ground celery seed
1 teaspoon ground cayenne pepper
1 teaspoon ground cumin

1. In a small bowl, combine the salt, pepper, onion powder, garlic powder, paprika, oregano, thyme, parsley, celery seed, cayenne, and cumin. 2. Apply evenly to all sides of meat 30 minutes to 3 hours before cooking.

Asian Butte-Ginger Sauce

Prep Time: 5 minutes | Cook Time: 2 minutes | Serves: 6

1 tablespoon toasted sesame oil
2 teaspoons peeled, minced fresh ginger
2 tablespoons oyster sauce

1 teaspoon soy sauce
¼ teaspoon mustard powder
¼ cup (½ stick) unsalted butter, cut into cubes

1. In a small skillet over medium heat, combine the oil and ginger and heat until the oil foams. 2. Remove from the heat and stir in the oyster sauce, soy sauce, and mustard. Whisk in the butter, a few cubes at a time, until incorporated.

Homemade Chipotle BBQ Sauce

Prep Time: 10 minutes | Cook Time: 10 minutes | Makes: 1 cup

1 cup ketchup
¼ cup white vinegar

¼ cup brown sugar
1 (4-ounce) can chipotle peppers in adobo sauce

1. In a blender or food processor, blend the ketchup, vinegar, sugar, and chipotle peppers until combined. 2. Pour the mixture into a small saucepan, bring to a boil, then reduce the heat to simmer for 5 minutes, stirring a few times. Store in airtight container and refrigerate for up to 3-to-4 days.

Flavorful Spicy Tomato Sauce

Prep Time: 10 minutes | Cook Time: 35 minutes | Serves: 6

1 tablespoon extra-virgin olive oil
1 cup finely chopped yellow onion
2 medium garlic cloves, minced
1 teaspoon crushed red pepper flakes

½ teaspoon dried oregano
1 can (28 ounces) crushed Italian plum tomatoes in juice
2 tablespoons tomato paste
1 teaspoon kosher salt

1. In a large, deep skillet over medium heat, warm the oil. Add the onion and sauté until tender but not golden, about 3 minutes. Add the garlic, pepper flakes, and oregano and cook until fragrant, about 1 minute, stirring often. Add the tomatoes and their juice, tomato paste, and salt and stir well. Cover partially and simmer until slightly thickened, about 30 minutes. 2. Remove from the heat and cover to keep warm. (The sauce can be made up to 4 days ahead. Let cool completely, then cover and refrigerate. Warm gently before serving.)

Thai-Red Curry Sauce

Prep Time: 10 minutes | Cook Time: 10 minutes | Serves: 6

1 tablespoon vegetable oil
1 tablespoon tomato paste
1 teaspoon minced garlic
½ teaspoon Thai red curry paste
1½ cups coconut milk
1 tablespoon fresh lime juice

1 teaspoon packed dark brown sugar
½ teaspoon ground turmeric
¼ teaspoon kosher salt
¼ teaspoon freshly ground black pepper
1 tablespoon finely chopped fresh basil or mint

1. In a saucepan over medium heat, warm the oil. Add the tomato paste, garlic, and curry paste and stir for 1 minute. 2. Add the rest of the ingredients except the basil and stir. Bring to a simmer and cook until the consistency of a cream sauce, 5 to 10 minutes, stirring occasionally. 3. Add the basil during the last minute, then remove from the heat. Set aside until ready to use.

Yummy Garlic-Thyme Butter

Prep Time: 10 minutes | Cook Time: 5 minutes | Serves: 6

4 tablespoons (½ stick) unsalted butter, divided
1 tablespoon minced garlic
¼ cup white wine

2 teaspoons sherry vinegar
2 teaspoons minced fresh thyme leaves
¼ teaspoon kosher salt

1. In a skillet over medium heat, melt 1 tablespoon of the butter. Sauté the garlic until it starts to brown, around 2 minutes. Add the wine and vinegar and simmer until the sauce reduces by half, about 2 minutes. 2. Remove from the heat. Cut the remaining butter into chunks and whisk into the wine mixture, a few chunks at a time. 3. Stir in the thyme and salt and use right away.

Refreshing Grapefruit-Basil Aioli
Prep Time: 10 minutes | Cook Time: 0 minutes | Serves: 6

¼ cup mayonnaise
1 tablespoon chopped fresh basil
1½ teaspoons finely grated grapefruit zest

2 teaspoons fresh grapefruit juice
1 teaspoon minced garlic
¼ teaspoon kosher salt

In a small bowl, combine all the ingredients and mix thoroughly.

Lime Jalapeño Mayo
Prep Time: 10 minutes | Cook Time: 0 minutes | Serves: 4

½ cup mayonnaise
1 jalapeño chile pepper, seeded and minced
1 tablespoon finely grated lime zest
1 tablespoon fresh lime juice

1 garlic clove, minced
¼ teaspoon ground cumin
¼ teaspoon kosher salt
¼ teaspoon freshly ground black pepper

In a small bowl, whisk together all the ingredients. Cover and refrigerate until needed.

Tangy Tomato Sauce

Prep Time: 5 minutes | Cook Time: 20 minutes | Makes: 3½ cups

1 tablespoon extra-virgin olive oil
2 garlic cloves, finely chopped
1 (28-ounce) can crushed tomatoes

10 fresh basil leaves
Kosher salt
Freshly ground black pepper

1. To install the grill grate, position it flat on top of the heating element so it sits in place. 2. Select the BAKE function. Adjust the temperature to 350°F and time to 1 minute. Select START/STOP to begin preheating. 3. When preheating is complete, open the hood. Pour the oil into a baking pan and place on the grill grate. Close the hood. Once hot, add the garlic. Close the hood and cook for 30 to 60 seconds or until the garlic is golden brown. 4. Add the tomatoes. Close the hood and cook, stirring once, until slightly thickened, about 20 minutes. 5. Remove the pan from the grill. Tear the basil leaves into the sauce. Season with salt and pepper. 6. Use immediately, or let cool and transfer to an airtight container. Refrigerate for up to 1 week.

Chapter 10 Desserts

Cinnamon Chocolate Sauce

Prep Time: 15 minutes | Cook Time: 20 minutes | Makes: 2 cups

1½ cups heavy cream
¾ cup semisweet chocolate chips

⅛ teaspoon cinnamon
Pinch cayenne pepper (optional)

1. To install the grill grate, position it flat on top of the heating element so it sits in place. 2. Select the BAKE function. Adjust the temperature to 250°F and time to 10 minutes. Select START/STOP to begin preheating. 3. Pour the cream and chocolate chips into a baking pan. 4. When preheating is complete, open the hood and place the baking pan on the grate. Once the hood is closed, cooking will begin and the timer will start counting down. 5. After 10 minutes, open the hood and give it a good stir. Cook for an additional 5 to 10 minutes. Once the chocolate has melted and has incorporated with the cream, remove and stir in the cinnamon and cayenne (if using). 6. Remove from the grill and serve immediately.

Lemon Peach Cobbler

Prep Time: 15 minutes | Cook Time: 1 hour | Serves: 8

4 cups sliced fresh or frozen peaches (thawed if frozen)
1 cup sugar, divided
Grated zest and juice of ½ lemon
1 teaspoon vanilla extract

1 teaspoon ground cinnamon
8 tablespoons (1 stick) unsalted butter, melted
1 cup all-purpose flour
1 tablespoon baking powder

1. To install grill grate, position it flat on top of the heating element so it sits in place, place a baking pan on the grill grate and close the hood. Use pellet scoop to pour pellets into smoke box until filled to top. 2. Select GRILL. Select WOODFIRE FLAVOR. Set grill temperature to HI. Set the time to 10 minutes. Select START/STOP to begin preheating. 3. When preheating is complete, open the hood. Put the peaches, ½ cup of sugar, the lemon zest and juice, vanilla, and cinnamon in the baking pan and stir to combine. Close the hood and cook, stirring occasionally, for 10 minutes or until the peaches soften and the sugar dissolves. Remove from the grill. 4. Reduce the grill to low heat. Pour the butter into a 10-inch cast iron skillet. 5. In a medium bowl, mix together the remaining ½ cup of sugar, flour, and the baking powder. Pour evenly over the butter, but do not stir. 6. Pour the peach mixture over the top of the flour mixture. Put the skillet on the grill grate. Close the hood and cook for 45 to 50 minutes or until the cobbler is golden brown on top. 7. Put on a wire rack to cool for 15 minutes before serving.

Pineapple & Cherry Upside-Down Cake

Prep Time: 10 minutes | Cook Time: 40 minutes | Serves: 12

1 (20-ounce) can crushed pineapple in 100% pineapple juice
2¼ cups all-purpose flour
1½ cups granulated sugar
3½ teaspoons baking powder
1 teaspoon salt
8 tablespoons (1 stick) unsalted butter, at room temperature, plus 4 tablespoons (½ stick), melted

1¼ cups whole milk
2 tablespoons vegetable oil
1 tablespoon vanilla extract
3 large eggs
1 cup packed light brown sugar
12 maraschino cherries

1. To install the grill grate, position it flat on top of the heating element so it sits in place. 2. Select the BAKE function. Adjust the temperature to 350°F and time to 20 minutes. Select START/STOP to begin preheating. 3. Pour the crushed pineapple into a strainer set over a bowl and push the pineapple down using the back of a spoon to remove most of the liquid. Reserve the pineapple juice. 4. In a medium bowl, whisk the flour, granulated sugar, baking powder, and salt. 5. Place 8 tablespoons (1 stick) of room-temperature butter into the bowl of a stand mixer fitted with the paddle attachment and beat on medium speed for 1 to 2 minutes, until creamy. Add the dry ingredients to the butter and beat for about 30 seconds until combined. Pour in the milk (replacing as much of the milk as possible with the reserved pineapple juice), oil, vanilla, and eggs. Beat on medium speed for 1 to 2 minutes, until fully incorporated. 6. Pour the tablespoons of melted butter into a by inch baking dish and fully coat the surface. Pour in the brown sugar and spread it evenly over the bottom of the dish. Spread the strained pineapple evenly over the brown sugar. Arrange the cherries in two rows of 6 cherries each. 7. Gently pour the cake batter over the pineapples and cherries. 8. When preheating is complete, open the hood and place the baking dish on the grate. Once the hood is closed, cooking will begin and the timer will start counting down. 9. Rotate the baking dish 180 degrees and cook for 20 minutes more. The cake is done when a butter knife inserted into the center comes out clean. 10. Immediately run a knife around the inside of the baking dish to loosen the cake. Place a large serving platter or cutting board upside down onto the baking dish and turn over the platter and dish together. Gently pull the baking dish straight up, releasing the cake. Let the cake cool for at least 1 hour before serving.

Best Apple Crisp

Prep Time: 25 minutes | Cook Time: 1 hour | Serves: 6

5 Granny Smith apples, peeled, cored, and thinly sliced
1 tablespoon freshly squeezed lemon juice
¼ cup brown sugar, plus ⅓ cup
2 tablespoons white sugar
3 tablespoons melted butter
2 teaspoons vanilla extract

¾ teaspoon ground cinnamon, divided
1¼ cups old-fashioned oats
¼ cup flour
5 tablespoons cold butter, chopped
¼ teaspoon ground nutmeg
Vegetable oil, for greasing

1. To install the grill grate, position it flat on top of the heating element so it sits in place. 2. Select the BAKE function. Adjust the temperature to 350°F and time to 1 hour. Select START/STOP to begin preheating. 3. In a large bowl, combine the apples, lemon juice, ¼ cup of brown sugar, white sugar, melted butter, vanilla, and ¼ teaspoon of cinnamon. Set aside. 4. In a food processor, combine the flour, oats, remaining ⅓ cup of brown sugar, cold butter, remaining ½ teaspoon of cinnamon, and nutmeg. Pulse 5 or 6 times. 5. Grease the inside of a baking pan with oil. Arrange the sliced apples in the bottom of the pan, then top with the crumble mixture. 6. When preheating is complete, open the hood and place the baking pan on the grate. Once the hood is closed, cooking will begin and the timer will start counting down. 7. Remove the pan and let cool for 15 minutes. Serve with a scoop of vanilla ice cream and a drizzle of warm caramel sauce.

Homemade Pineapple Upside-Down Cake

Prep Time: 30 minutes | Cook Time: 52 minutes | Serves: 8

Topping:
6 slices peeled, cored fresh pineapple, each ½ inch thick
2 tablespoons unsalted butter, melted
½ cup packed dark brown sugar
Batter:
1 cup unbleached all-purpose flour
1 teaspoon baking powder
½ teaspoon kosher salt
¼ teaspoon baking soda
⅔ cup buttermilk

¼ cup heavy whipping cream
½ teaspoon ground cinnamon

2 large eggs
1 teaspoon vanilla extract
½ cup (1 stick) unsalted butter, softened
¾ cup granulated sugar

1. To install the grill grate, position it flat on top of the heating element so it sits in place. 2. Select the BAKE function. Adjust the temperature to 400°F and time to 5 minutes. Select START/STOP to begin preheating. 3. Brush the pineapple rings on both sides with the butter. 4. When preheating is complete, open the hood and place the pineapple rings on the grate. Once the hood is closed, cooking will begin and the timer will start counting down, turning once. Remove from the grill and let cool. Leave one ring whole and cut the others in half. 5. In a baking pan, mix together the brown sugar, cream, cinnamon, and any remaining butter from brushing the pineapple slices. Position the pan on the grill grate and close the hood. Bake at 400°F until the sugar is melted and the liquid begins to bubble around the outer edge of the pan, approximately 2 minutes. Remove the pan from the grill and place the whole pineapple slice in the center of the pan and arrange the halved pineapple slices around it. Set aside. 6. In a bowl, stir together the flour, baking powder, salt, and baking soda. In a second bowl whisk together the buttermilk, eggs, and vanilla. In a medium bowl, using an electric mixer, cream the butter and sugar on medium-high speed until lightened, 2 to 4 minutes. On low speed, add the buttermilk mixture and beat until mixed. Gradually add the flour mixture and beat until smooth, scraping down the sides of the bowl as needed. Spread the batter evenly over the pineapple slices. 7. Place the pan on the grate and bake at 350°F for 45 minutes, until the top is golden brown and a skewer inserted into the center comes out clean. Remove from the grill and let cool for about 10 minutes. 8. Run a paring knife around the inside edge of the pan, then carefully invert the pan and cake onto a platter. Gently lift the pan off the grill and loosen any pineapple slices that may have stuck to the bottom of the skillet, placing them back on top of the cake. Allow the cake to cool briefly before slicing it into wedges and serving. For optimal taste and texture, enjoy the cake warm or at room temperature on the day it is baked.

Delicious S'mores

Prep Time: 5 minutes | Cook Time: 5 minutes | Serves: 8

12 ounces semisweet baking chocolate, coarsely chopped
4 cups miniature marshmallows

Graham crackers

1. To install the grill grate, position it flat on top of the heating element so it sits in place. 2. Select the BAKE function. Adjust the temperature to 450°F and time to 5 minutes. Select START/STOP to begin preheating. 3. Sprinkle the chocolate evenly in the bottom of a baking pan. Cover the chocolate with the marshmallows. 4. When preheating is complete, open the hood and place the baking pan on the grate. Once the hood is closed, cooking will begin and the timer will start counting down. Bake until the marshmallows are browned, about 5 minutes. 5. Remove the pan from the grill and let stand for 5 minutes. Serve with the graham crackers, using them to dip into the skillet.

Homemade Candied Pineapple

Prep Time: 15 minutes | Cook Time: 1 hour | Serves: 6

1 pineapple
½ cup dark rum
1 cup light brown sugar

1½ teaspoons ground cinnamon
½ teaspoon ground nutmeg

1. Cut the stem and skin off the pineapple, making it as close to a rectangular shape as possible. 2. Put the rum into a small bowl or cup. Draw some of it into the injector and slowly inject it into the pineapple in different sections, starting with the core and working around it. 3. In a small bowl, combine the brown sugar, cinnamon, and nutmeg. 4. Place the pineapple in a large aluminum pan and coat the top with half of the sugar mixture. 5. To install the grill grate, position it flat on top of the heating element so it sits in place. 6. Select the BAKE function. Adjust the temperature to 350°F and time to 30 minutes. Select START/STOP to begin preheating. 7. When preheating is complete, open the hood and place the pan on the grill grate. Once the hood is closed, cooking will begin and the timer will begin counting down. 8. Using heat-resistant gloves, carefully turn the pineapple over and sprinkle the remaining half of the sugar mixture on the opposite side. Close the hood and continue to cook for 30 more minutes. The pineapple will have a nice brown color and caramelization on its surface when done. 9. Remove and let it rest for 5 minutes. Transfer to a cutting board and slice into 1-inch-thick rounds. Serve with ice cream on top.

Soft Ginger Cake

Prep Time: 5 minutes | Cook Time: 1 hour | Serves: 8

1 cup (2 sticks) unsalted butter, cubed, plus more for the pan, at room temperature
2½ cups all-purpose flour
2½ teaspoons baking powder
4 teaspoons ground ginger

1 teaspoon kosher salt
1⅔ cups packed light brown sugar
4 large eggs
½ cup whole milk

1. To install the grill grate, position it flat on top of the heating element so it sits in place. 2. Select the BAKE function. Adjust the temperature to 350°F and time to 1 hour. Select START/STOP to begin preheating. 3. Butter the bottom and sides of a baking pan. 4. In a medium bowl, mix together the flour, baking powder, ginger, and salt. 5. In the bowl of an electric mixer, cream together the butter and sugar on medium speed for 3 minutes. 6. Lower the speed to medium-low and incorporate the eggs one at a time, mixing for 1 to 2 minutes or until they turn light tan in color. 7. Then, while the machine is still running, pour in the milk. 8. Incorporate the flour mixture into the batter, ensuring to scrape down the sides of the bowl as needed, until fully combined. Then, transfer the batter to the pan. Transfer to the pan. 9. When preheating is complete, open the hood and place the baking pan on the grate. Once the hood is closed, cooking will begin and the timer will start counting down. Bake until a knife inserted into the center comes out clean. 10. Put on a wire rack to cool completely before serving.

Chocolate Bread Pudding

Prep Time: 20 minutes | Cook Time: 55 minutes | Serves: 8

2 tablespoons unsalted butter, cut into small pieces, at room temperature, plus more for greasing the pan
4 cups cubed day-old bread (from about 12 inches of baguette)
6 ounces bittersweet chocolate baking chips
1½ teaspoons ground cardamom

2 cups whole milk
¾ cup heavy cream
2 large eggs
¼ cup packed light brown sugar

1. Butter the bottom and sides of a baking pan; arrange the bread in a single layer in it. 2. Set up a double boiler: Fill a small saucepan with about 1 inch of water and place a bowl on top (make sure it does not touch the water). Put the chocolate in the bowl and bring the water to a boil over high heat on the stove top to melt the chocolate. Stir in the cardamom. 3. Meanwhile, in a medium saucepan, heat the milk and cream over medium-high heat on the stove top just until it comes to a simmer. Remove from the heat. 4. In a small bowl, whisk the eggs and sugar together. Slowly add ½ cup of the hot milk mixture to the bowl, then pour the egg mixture into the saucepan. Cook over medium heat, whisking constantly, for 30 to 60 seconds or until it coats the back of a spatula and a streak can be drawn through it. Remove from the heat. 5. Whisk in the chocolate until thoroughly combined. Pour over the bread in the pan. Let sit for 15 minutes (and up to 30 minutes) to allow the bread to absorb the flavors. Dot the top with the butter. 6. To install the grill grate, position it flat on top of the heating element so it sits in place. 7. Select the BAKE function. Adjust the temperature to 300°F and time to 40 minutes. Select START/STOP to begin preheating. 8. When preheating is complete, open the hood and place the baking pan on the grate. Once the hood is closed, cooking will begin and the timer will start counting down. Bake until a knife inserted into the center comes out clean. 9. Put on a wire rack to cool for 15 minutes before serving.

Flavorful Pumpkin Pie

Prep Time: 5 minutes | Cook Time: 40 minutes | Serves: 8

1 (15-ounce) can pure pumpkin purée
2 large eggs, beaten
⅓ cup packed light brown sugar
1 tablespoon ground cinnamon

2 teaspoons ground allspice
½ teaspoon ground cloves
1 (9-inch) graham cracker pie shell

1. To install the grill grate, position it flat on top of the heating element so it sits in place. 2. Select the BAKE function. Adjust the temperature to 350°F and time to 40 minutes. Select START/STOP to begin preheating. 3. In a large bowl, whisk together the pumpkin purée, eggs, sugar, cinnamon, allspice, and cloves until smooth and thoroughly combined. Pour into the pie shell. 4. When preheating is complete, open the hood and place the pie on the grate. Once the hood is closed, cooking will begin and the timer will start counting down. 5. Put on a wire rack to cool completely before serving.

Banana Chocolate Sundaes

Prep Time: 15 minutes | Cook Time: 5 minutes | Serves: 6

Sauce:
½ cup heavy whipping cream
3 ounces semisweet chocolate, finely chopped
¼ cup (½ stick) unsalted butter
½ teaspoon ground cinnamon

¼ teaspoon ground ginger
⅛ teaspoon ground cloves
4 ripe but firm bananas, peeled
1-pint vanilla ice cream

1. In a small saucepan over medium-high heat on the stove, bring the cream to a simmer. Remove the pan from the heat and immediately add the chocolate. Stir until the chocolate melts and the mixture is dark and smooth. Set aside. 2. In a large skillet over medium heat on the stove, melt the butter. Add the cinnamon, ginger, and cloves and stir to mix. Take the skillet off the heat, then place the bananas in it, ensuring to coat them on all sides with the butter mixture using a brush. 3. To install the grill grate, position it flat on top of the heating element so it sits in place. 4. Select the BAKE function. Adjust the temperature to 400°F and time to 2 minutes. Select START/STOP to begin preheating. 5. Gently pick the bananas out of the skillet. 6. When preheating is complete, open the hood and place the bananas on the grate or place bake pan on the grate. Once the hood is closed, cooking will begin and the timer will start counting down, gently turning once. Transfer the bananas to a cutting board and cut crosswise on the diagonal into ½-inch-thick slices. 7. Reheat the chocolate sauce over medium heat on the stove. In dessert bowls or sundae glasses, layer the ice cream, warm banana slices and chocolate sauce. Serve immediately.

Raisins Stuffed Apples

Prep Time: 10 minutes | Cook Time: 45 minutes | Serves: 6

6 Golden Delicious or Rome apples
6 tablespoons dark brown sugar
1½ teaspoons ground cinnamon
6 tablespoons raisins

6 tablespoons chopped walnuts (optional)
6 teaspoons cold unsalted butter, cut into 1-teaspoon slices
¾ cup boiling water
Vanilla bean ice cream, for serving (optional)

1. To install the grill grate, position it flat on top of the heating element so it sits in place. 2. Select the BAKE function. Adjust the temperature to 375°F and time to 45 minutes. Select START/STOP to begin preheating. 3. Wash and dry the apples thoroughly. With a sharp paring knife or an apple corer, carefully remove the cores, ensuring to leave about half an inch of the bottom of the apple intact. Then, using a teaspoon, scoop out the seeds, creating a one-inch-wide cavity through the center of the apple. 4. In a small bowl, stir together the brown sugar, cinnamon, raisins, and walnuts (if using). Using a teaspoon, stuff the apples with the brown sugar mixture. Place a slice of butter on top of the sugar mixture in each apple. 5. Place the apples in a baking dish and pour the boiling water into the bottom of the dish, so it wets the bottoms of the apples. 6. When preheating is complete, open the hood and place the baking dish on the grate. Once the hood is closed, cooking will begin and the timer will start counting down. Bake until they are cooked through and tender. When the apples are done, baste them with the juice from the baking dish. 7. Serve each apple with a scoop of vanilla ice cream (if using).

Mixed Berries Crisp

Prep Time: 15 minutes | Cook Time: 40 minutes | Serves: 8

2 pounds frozen mixed berries
¼ cup granulated sugar
⅓ cup freshly squeezed orange juice
⅔ cup all-purpose flour
¾ teaspoon baking powder
⅛ teaspoon kosher salt

8 tablespoons (1 stick) unsalted butter, melted
½ cup packed light brown sugar
½ teaspoon vanilla extract
1 large egg
Whipped cream or whipped topping

1. To install the grill grate, position it flat on top of the heating element so it sits in place. 2. Select the BAKE function. Adjust the temperature to 350°F and time to 20 minutes. Select START/STOP to begin preheating. 3. In a medium bowl, stir together the berries, granulated sugar, and orange juice. Pour the berry mixture into baking pan. In another medium bowl, whisk the flour, baking powder, and salt. 4. In another medium bowl, using an electric hand mixer, cream together the melted butter and brown sugar. Add the vanilla and egg and mix until fully incorporated. Slowly add the flour mixture and stir with a wooden spoon until incorporated but not overmixed. 5. Using a tablespoon, spoon the batter over the berries, dropping it in small clumps and leaving gaps between the batter, so the berries peek through. 6. When preheating is complete, open the hood and place the baking pan on the grate. Once the hood is closed, cooking will begin and the timer will start counting down. 7. Rotate the pan 180 degrees and cook for 20 minutes more. The crisp is done when the batter is golden brown and the berry mixture is bubbling. Remove the pan from the grill and serve the hot crisp with whipped cream.

Cherry Hand Pies

Prep Time: 15 minutes | Cook Time: 15 minutes | Serves: 12

1 (14-ounce) package refrigerated (not frozen in the tin) piecrust (contains 2 piecrusts)
1 (21-ounce) can cherry pie filling
1 large egg white, beaten

2½ cups powdered sugar
1 teaspoon freshly squeezed lemon juice
¼ cup whole milk

1. Line a baking sheet with parchment paper. 2. To install the grill grate, position it flat on top of the heating element so it sits in place. 3. Select the BAKE function. Adjust the temperature to 425°F and time to 15 minutes. Select START/STOP to begin preheating. 4. Unroll the piecrusts and use a 4-inch biscuit cutter to cut 6 circles from each crust, for a total of 12 circles (you may need to reroll the dough scraps to get the final circle from each crust). 5. Drop 1 tablespoon of cherry pie filling into the center of each piecrust circle. Fold the piecrust circles in half and pinch the edges closed completely. Press the edges with the tines of a fork to seal. Poke the hand pie once through the top only with the fork; the small holes will prevent the pie from bursting. 6. Place the hand pies on the prepared baking sheet about 1 inch apart. Brush the tops of the hand pies with the beaten egg white. 7. When preheating is complete, open the hood and place the baking sheet on the grate. Once the hood is closed, cooking will begin and the timer will start counting down. Bake until the crusts are golden brown. 8. In a medium bowl, whisk the powdered sugar lemon juice and milk until smooth. 9. Remove the hand pies from the grill, then carefully drop one hand pie into the icing mixture. Use two forks to remove it from the icing and return it to the parchment paper. Repeat with the remaining pies. Alternatively, put the icing in a zip-top bag, cut a hole in one of the corners, and drizzle the icing onto the hand pies. Let the icing set for 5 minutes before serving.

Roasted Strawberry Ice Cream

Prep Time: 10 minutes | Cook Time: 10 minutes | Serves: 8

2 pints' large strawberries (20 to 24 berries)
¼ cup granulated sugar
¼ cup orange-flavored liqueur, or 2 tablespoons water and 1 tablespoon fresh lemon juice

½ teaspoon vanilla extract
1 tablespoon unsalted butter, softened
Vanilla ice cream

1. Remove the stems from the strawberries, then trim the flat end of each berry. In a medium bowl, mix together the berries, sugar, liqueur, and vanilla, ensuring they are evenly coated. Next, generously spread butter over the bottom and sides of a baking pan. The pan should be sized just right to accommodate the berries in a single layer, with their sides almost touching. 3. To install grill grate, position it flat on top of the heating element so it sits in place, then close hood. 4. Select ROAST. Set the temperature to 500°F. Set the time to 10 minutes. Select START/STOP to begin preheating. 5. Remove the berries from the bowl and stand them in a single layer, flat side down and almost touching, in the prepared pan. Pour any liquid remaining in the bottom of the bowl evenly over the berries. 6. When preheating is complete, place the pan on the grill grate. Close hood and grill for 10 minutes. 7. Remove the pan from the grill and spoon the pan juices over the berries to moisten them. Let cool for 5 minutes, then carefully cut the berries into quarters or leave whole. Scoop ice cream into individual dessert bowls and spoon the berries and juices over the ice cream. Serve right away.

The "NINJA WOODFIRE Pro XL OUTDOOR GRILL" comes with 7 cooking functions such as grill, smoke, air crisp, bake, roast, broil, and dehydrate, and 5 operating buttons such as dial, temperature, time, start/stop, and woodfire flavor technology, and essential accessories such as grill grate, crisper basket, smoke box, pellet scoop, control panel, hood, and assemble handles. This cooking appliance has a grilled option for indoor grilling food. You can grill food into your kitchen. If you choose my cookbook, your choice is perfect because we added all details about this cooking appliance. You didn't need to go outside for grilling food. In my cookbook, I added delicious, mouthwatering, and healthy recipes for you and your family. You didn't need to buy another appliance for cooking food because it has 7 useful cooking functions in one pot. You can prepare your favorite food on different occasions. Thank you for choosing my book. I hope you love and appreciate my book. This appliance has a large capacity, and you can prepare a large amount of food for your big family. Read a book, appreciate it, and enjoy recipes!

Appendix 1 Measurement Conversion Chart

VOLUME EQUIVALENTS (LIQUID)

US STANDARD	US STANDARD (OUNCES)	METRIC (APPROXIMATE)
2 tablespoons	1 fl.oz	30 mL
¼ cup	2 fl.oz	60 mL
½ cup	4 fl.oz	120 mL
1 cup	8 fl.oz	240 mL
1½ cup	12 fl.oz	355 mL
2 cups or 1 pint	16 fl.oz	475 mL
4 cups or 1 quart	32 fl.oz	1 L
1 gallon	128 fl.oz	4 L

VOLUME EQUIVALENTS (DRY)

US STANDARD	METRIC (APPROXIMATE)
⅛ teaspoon	0.5 mL
¼ teaspoon	1 mL
½ teaspoon	2 mL
¾ teaspoon	4 mL
1 teaspoon	5 mL
1 tablespoon	15 mL
¼ cup	59 mL
½ cup	118 mL
¾ cup	177 mL
1 cup	235 mL
2 cups	475 mL
3 cups	700 mL
4 cups	1 L

TEMPERATURES EQUIVALENTS

FAHRENHEIT(F)	CELSIUS(C) (APPROXIMATE)
225 °F	107 °C
250 °F	120 °C
275 °F	135 °C
300 °F	150 °C
325 °F	160 °C
350 °F	180 °C
375 °F	190 °C
400 °F	205 °C
425 °F	220 °C
450 °F	235 °C
475 °F	245 °C
500 °F	260 °C

WEIGHT EQUIVALENTS

US STANDARD	METRIC (APPROXINATE)
1 ounce	28 g
2 ounces	57 g
5 ounces	142 g
10 ounces	284 g
15 ounces	425 g
16 ounces (1 pound)	455 g
1.5 pounds	680 g
2 pounds	907 g

Appendix 2 Recipes Index

Made in United States
Orlando, FL
08 December 2024

55139669R00062